TEN GIRLS WHO DIDN'T GIVE IN

LIGHT KEEPERS

Irene Howat

© copyright 2004 Christian Focus Publications
Reprinted 2005

ISBN: 1-84550-036-9

Published by Christian Focus Publications Ltd,
Geanies House, Fearn, Tain, Ross-shire,
IV20 1TW, Scotland, Great Britain.
www.christianfocus.com
email:info@christianfocus.com

Cover design by Alister Macinnes
Cover illustration by Elena Temporin
Milan Illustrations Agency

All incidents retold in these stories are based on true situations. Where specific information about childhood incidents has been unobtainable the author has written these paragraphs using other information concerning family life, hobbies, home life, relationships freely available in other biographies.

Printed and bound
by
Nørhaven Paperback A/S, Denmark.

Dedication
for Dionne and Katherine Ann

Contents

Blandina

Two girls stood together at the well with their mother. She was waiting to draw water for her mistress, and the children were there because they were still too small to work.

'Run and play while I draw the water,' the woman said, 'because we'll have to get home quickly as soon as I've had my turn at the well.'

Blandina touched her friend on the arm.

'Tag!' she said, and then ran off.

The other child recognised the game immediately, though she wasn't best pleased that Blandina wanted to play tag.

'It's no fun chasing someone who can't run nearly as fast as you,' she thought. 'I could catch her every time, and sometimes I need to slow down and pretend I can't run any faster.'

But, having grumped to herself, the girl immediately perked up and played the game. After all, it wasn't every day that the children of slaves were free to have a runabout.

'It's my turn next!' Blandina's mother shouted to the girls. 'Watch to see when I've drawn the water and be ready to come right away.'

The woman before her filled two wooden pails with water then staggered off under the weight of them. Blandina's mother, who was a strong and healthy young woman, filled her pails in no time, and when she lowered the second one to the ground the girls were right there beside it.

'You are good, the pair of you,' said the slave woman. 'One of the other mothers had to go and look for her son then drag him back home! Now, off we go.'

It was quite a long walk from the well, and the sun was beating down on them.

'I wish it wasn't so hot,' said Blandina. 'I'm going to melt into a little grease spot on the ground.'

Her mother smiled, and thought of something interesting to tell the children to stop them slowing down.

'Did you know that there are parts of the Roman Empire that are much hotter than it is here in Lyon? Gaul (that's modern day France) is in between the hot Roman Empire and the cold Roman Empire.'

'Where is it coolest?' Blandina asked.

'Well,' said her mother, 'your father was talking to some soldiers who were passing through Lyon on their way home to Rome. They had been serving the Emperor in the north of England, and they said it was cold there and that it rained nearly all the time!'

'Why does the Emperor put his soldiers as far away as that?' queried the child.

'Apparently he had them building a wall right across England to show the people who was in charge!'

'And where's the hottest part of the Empire?' the other girl asked.

They were nearly home now, and almost running in case they were seen and thought to be slacking.

'I think that will be Rome itself,' said the slave woman. 'I've heard it's a fearfully hot place in the summer.'

As soon as they went into the courtyard the children disappeared as though they had indeed melted into grease spots on the ground. Slave children learned to do disappearing acts. It was the best way to keep out of trouble.

'I'm worried about Blandina,' her mother said that night, when the girl was sound asleep. 'Do you think she's a healthy child?'

Her husband looked concerned.

'She seems healthy enough. But she's not what I'd call strong. Although she tries hard, she does run out of energy before other girls her age. But that's probably because she's smaller than they are.'

'I'm worried that she won't grow,' said the woman. 'There's no place in this hard world for a slave girl who can't pull her weight when there's work to be done.'

'You're worrying too soon,' her husband decided. 'She'll put on height and then she'll strengthen up. You wait and see.'

'She's not even what you'd call a pretty girl,' said the woman, who was in a mood for sharing her troubles.

But as her husband was not in a mood for listening, that was as far as the conversation went.

Blandina's mother did wait, but she did not see very much of a difference. True, her daughter grew, but she grew into a spindly sort of a girl. She was very willing to work, and so far her owner didn't seem to have noticed that she hadn't much muscle about her. That was a comfort to her mother, but it didn't stop her worrying.

'Now listen to me,' she told Blandina, when she was beginning to grow up. 'When the mistress is around, always, always be busy. Don't ever be seen standing doing nothing. I know you sometimes feel worn out and need a rest, but just be sure you take your rests out of sight of the mistress. She won't want to buy food for a slave that's not earning her keep.'

Advice like that was necessary in those days, but it had the effect of making Blandina feel nervous and on edge. She kept watching to the side and behind herself just to make sure that she was working hard enough when she was within sight of anyone who mattered.

By the time Blandina was almost an adult, she was a servant cum slave to a Christian woman. We don't know how that came about, but could it have been that the woman felt sorry for the girl?

'She's a timid girl and not strong,' the Christian lady told her sister, 'but have you looked at her face? It's not a handsome face, but she has character.' Then as an afterthought, she added, 'She has a kind of strength of character that you don't see in many girls her age.'

Was it through working for a Christian that Blandina was converted? We don't know. But we do know that while she was still in her teens she learned about the Lord Jesus Christ and became one of his followers. When she was able to meet with the other Christians in Lyon, her mistress was also one of the congregation!

It was during one of these meetings that Blandina caught her mistress's eye, and a smile went between them that the girl thought she would always remember.

11

'One of the men was reading God's Word,' she told another slave girl as they settled down to sleep that night. 'He read wonderful words that I'd never heard before. He said that those who are followers of Jesus are all alike in his eyes, that God doesn't see Jews different from Greeks, or men different from women ...'

Her friend's eyes were closing with exhaustion and Blandina nudged her to hear the best bit of all. But the girl was shocked into total wakefulness by what Blandina said next.

'... and he said that God doesn't see slaves any different from people who are free!'

'Do you believe that?' her friend asked.

'I do!' said Blandina. 'And I'm sure the mistress believes it too for, when the preacher said it, she looked round at me and smiled!'

'Tell Blandina to come and help me,' the mistress told one of her slaves. 'She does things how I want them done.'

As time passed this happened more and more often until the two women were in each other's company quite a lot of the time. Sometimes the older woman even read from the Bible to her slave! Yet more surprising, there were times when her mistress asked Blandina to pray for her. The first time that happened the girl almost jumped in surprise...

and perhaps in fear. Things that were out of the ordinary could still make the young woman feel nervous.

'These are troubled times,' the preacher told his congregation one Sunday. 'The Emperor Marcus Aurelius has no time for Christians. Since he became Emperor (in 161 AD) vicious things have happened to believers. And I have news for you, brothers and sisters, the noose is tightening around Lyon. I believe that the persecutions are coming here, and that some of you might even have to die for the Lord.'

On hearing what he said, Blandina's first reaction was to enjoy the warm feeling that she always experienced when the preacher called the congregation 'brothers and sisters'. She was a slave, away from her family, but the little church in Lyon was her family in a very real way. Then the rest of the message sank into her head.

'Some of you might even have to die for the Lord ...'

Looking round the congregation she saw fine, tall, strong young men – most of them slaves like herself – and she wondered it they would be first to be rounded up and tried.

'But why should they be?' she asked herself, as she walked home alone. 'The Roman soldiers could arrest me as easily as them.'

Then she stopped in her tracks. 'My mistress! Surely they'll not arrest my mistress! Surely they'll only take slaves ...'

When the whole force of Marcus Aurelius's anger was unleashed, he didn't care whether Christians were slaves or free, he just wanted them killed in the most horrible and public ways possible.

'We must pray for each other, you and me,' her mistress told Blandina, when news of terrible happenings reached them. 'We're sisters in Jesus and we must help each other as best we can.'

Blandina looked at her mistress. 'How strong you are,' she thought admiringly, 'and how brave. If the soldiers arrested you, you would walk to the prison with your head held high.'

And looking at her servant, the woman thought just the opposite. 'What a frail young woman you are. And I wonder how you'll cope when we're arrested, as I'm sure we will be. I'll do everything I can for you.'

The Emperor's anger raged hot and centred itself on Lyon. Roman soldiers did a great sweep of Christians and many, including Blandina and her mistress, were thrown into prison. In her cell the young woman looked even more frail and more nervous than she did at home.

'Pray for Blandina,' her mistress whispered to the other Christians one at a time. 'Pray that God will give her the courage to bear what's going to happen. Pray that she'll not deny the Lord Jesus just to be set free.'

14

The next morning the prison guard barged in and went to drag Blandina out to trial. But she didn't need to be dragged. She went willingly, with her head held high. All day the prisoners wondered what was happening to her, and they were amazed when they heard the news. Blandina had endured so much torture that her torturers had given up in exhaustion!

'My dear child,' her mistress said, when the young woman's broken body was returned to the cell overnight. 'My dearest child.'

Her loving words were like cool water to Blandina, who fell asleep in her arms.

The following day the same thing happened. The slave girl was taken from the cell and accused of terrible things.

'I'm a Christian,' she said over, and over again. 'And we've done nothing evil.'

Her torture went on all day. Once again she was returned to her cell where her mistress waited to soothe her wounds and pray with her. The following day Blandina was taken to the amphitheatre with three other Christians to be fed to wild beasts.

Those left in the cells prayed as they'd never prayed before. At first the beasts didn't go in Blandina's direction, but eventually her tormentors were satisfied she was dead. What they didn't know was that the one they had just killed was alive in heaven, and happier at that very moment that she'd ever been on earth!

The number of Christians meeting to worship God the following Sunday was much smaller than it had been the previous week.

'Brothers and sisters,' the preacher said. 'This has been a terrible and a wonderful week for us. We have seen many of our members pass from death to glory, and that is both terrible and wonderful. Not only that, but we have seen an example of such Christian courage as will be remembered a thousand years from now. Our little sister, the timid and weak Blandina, showed herself to have courage and strength that could only have come from the Lord. In her death she was an example to us that one day we may need to follow. If we should be called on to be martyrs for Jesus, may we be just like our sister Blandina.'

'Amen and Amen,' said every single person there.

It is over 1800 years since Blandina died rather than deny her Saviour. Her name is to be found in just a few pages of some very old books. But it is good to begin a new book with her story, and to keep her name alive into the 21st century. This book tells the stories of ten girls who gave up their lives for Jesus. May they be shining examples to us to live our lives for the Lord.

Factfile

 Gaul: The natives of the area where Blandina lived would not have called it Gaul. That was the name given to it by the Romans who conquered it in stages from 222 - 51 BC. The part that Blandina lived in was conquered in the last stage (between 58 and 51 BC) by Julius Caesar. He wrote a famous book about his conquests called 'The Gallic Wars'. The people who originally lived in Gaul were Celts, who spoke a language related to modern day Welsh or Gaelic. As the Roman Empire began to collapse in the eest, they gradually lost control of Gaul. But it was conquered again by tribes such as the Franks that came in from east of Gaul.

 Keynote: Blandina might not have been as strong or as fast as other girls, but that did not mean that God did not want her. Even though she was weak physically, God gave her great strength so she could bear torture and not deny her Lord. This is still true. God doesn't always choose to use big strong people. The Bible tells us that his strength is made perfect in our weakness (Phil. 4:13).

Think: It was not the custom for a slave's mistress to say anything to her except for instructions. However, Blandina's mistress did not behave that way because she knew that God did not see slaves and free people differently. The Bible tells us that we should not behave differently to rich and poor people either (James 2:1-10). Think about how you can make sure that you do not show favouritism towards the people you meet.

Prayer: Lord Jesus, thank you for accepting sinners like me, whether or not we are big, strong or popular. Help me to love you as I should, and not to show favouritism. Amen

Perpetua

It was a warm and sunny day in the city of Carthage in North Africa. And it was just the time of day when people rested from the sun. Perpetua was glad to rest.

'My head is going to burst,' she told her friend. 'One day my teacher spends hours doing Latin and the next we spend hours doing Greek. Sometime I'm going to open my mouth and not know which language to speak!'

'It's mathematics that I find difficult,' her friend complained. 'All those shapes and lines and angles.'

Perpetua laughed. 'If I help you with your mathematics you could help me with my language work.'

The other girl giggled. 'That sounds a good idea.'

Just then a slave arrived with freshly squeezed orange juice for the girls. As they relaxed in the shade enjoying their drinks, Perpetua noticed that the slave girl was working in the full glare of the sun. Having squeezed fruit to make drinks for all the family, she was now back at her job of milling wheat for bread.

'She doesn't have to bother about either mathematics or Latin or Greek,' said the visiting teenager.

But when Perpetua looked at the sweating child, who was only about ten years old, she knew that however hard schoolwork was it was easier than being a slave.

'I'd rather be me,' she told her friend. 'Or perhaps I'd rather have lived in earlier days, or in another country, where only boys are educated. It's jolly hard work being a girl in Carthage today.'

'The sun's going down now,' Perpetua said. 'Let's get my young brother and play a game.'

Summoning her slave, the teenager explained what she wanted. 'Bring my brother, and bring cloth so that we can dress up and pretend to be goddesses.'

The slave ran as fast as she could to the house and was back in no time at all. One arm was full of fabric, and the other was full of protesting boy.

'I didn't want to come outside to play,' the eight-year-old complained. 'I can't be bothered.'

The two girls were not really interested in whether he could be bothered or not, even though they knew his lack of energy was because he was ill. In fact, it suited the game quite well that after the lad was dressed in white he lounged around under a tree.

'Imagine he's one of the gods watching us pretty girls playing,' said Perpetua. 'Let's dance to please him. Dad says we should always be finding ways to please the gods or they'll turn nasty on us.'

'Let's dress up as priestesses of the god Ceres,' suggested Perpetua, 'and pretend that my brother is Saturn. That'll be fun.'

Gathering the cloth around them, they prepared for their roles. And the dance the two priestesses of Ceres danced for Saturn was very elegant indeed. But the little boy hardly bothered with their dancing at all. He lay on the grass under the tree and watched the sunlight through the leaves. And by the next time her friend came to visit, Perpetua's little brother had died of the disease that had weakened him for so long.

Did her little brother's death make Perpetua wonder what good all the gods did, or did it make her wonder if the Christian God was real after all? Nobody knows, for the next few years of her life have been lost from the pages of history. The next time she is heard of, Perpetua is a young married woman with a tiny baby boy of her own. And she's a Christian! We have to guess how that happened, but our guesses join up with facts when she was 22 years old. We know the girl wasn't brought up in a Christian home, so she must have heard about the Lord Jesus elsewhere. Some of the Christians in Carthage at the time (it was just under 200 years after Jesus was born) were slaves. It may be that her father bought a slave who told her about the Lord. Or she might have heard the gospel spoken about in the city. Jesus really was the talk of the town because of what happened to some of those who believed in him.

Fast-forwarding Perpetua's life takes us to her 23rd year and a diary she kept of what happened to her. A friend who finished her story completed the diary. At that time Christians in Carthage had relative freedom, and only very occasionally did the Romans feel a need to make martyrs of them. The Roman Emperor, Septimus Severus, decided that one such time had come, and his Proconsul in Carthage carried out his orders.

'The Christians are disloyal to our gods,' he told his advisors. 'And if they anger the gods there's no saying what they'll do to us. Angry gods don't make good friends.'

'But do we need to kill the Christians?' one of the men asked.

The Proconsul stamped his foot. 'Of course we don't! All they need to do is offer incense to our gods to keep them in a good mood, then

24

we can set them free... till the next time. Take that young Perpetua,' the Proconsul went on. 'Why anyone from her background wants to get involved with slaves who make up most of the Christians here I really don't know. Bring her in and we'll sort her out. And bring her friends with her.'

So it was that a small group of young Christians were arrested: several youths, along with Perpetua and another girl about her own age. She was called Felicitas, and she was a slave. They knew each other from church.

'You're summoned to appear before the Proconsul's court!' the Christians were told.

The young people prayed then followed the guard without looking back. Their trial came to an end when the prisoners refused to sacrifice to the Roman gods.

'If you don't make sacrifices to them,' the Proconsul warned, 'you will be sacrificed to them.'

There was no misunderstanding what the man meant, but none of the young folk as much as flinched. In fact, they thought that giving up their lives for Jesus was the best thing in the world they could do.

The prospect of dying didn't seem to trouble Perpetua much at all, but two things did upset her – the thought of giving up her baby son before the day of her death, and

25

the horrible state of the prison. Having been brought up in a wealthy home, she found the filthy prison hard to endure. But that night her mind was far from her prison, as God gave her a vision of heaven, a vision that showed her that she would soon be martyred for her faith.

'After a few days there was a report that we were to have a court hearing,' Perpetua wrote in a diary that was found many years later. 'My father came to the hearing, bringing my baby son with him. "Have pity on me, my daughter!" he cried. "Have pity on your father. I brought you up to become what you are. You are my favourite. Think of me, or your brothers, your mother and aunt. And think of your son! Just tell them you're not a Christian and they'll set you free." As he spoke, my father kissed my hands then threw himself at my feet, begging me to do what I needed to do to be sent free.'

'I looked at my father,' she wrote on, then pointed to a jug that was close by him. '"What would you call that?" I asked him. "It's a jug," he replied. "Would you not call it by another name?" I asked. "No," Father said. "I can't call it anything other than what it is. And it's a jug." So I said to my father, "I am a Christian. I can't call myself anything else because that is what I am."'

Perpetua and her friends were returned to prison. But they didn't go alone as she was allowed to take her infant son with her.

'It's a strange thing,' Felicitas said, as they sat together in prison, 'but we are brothers and sisters together in the Lord, even though I'm a slave and you were born free.'

'That's what the Bible means when it says that we are all one in Christ Jesus,' agreed Perpetua. 'And now it looks as though we are going to end our lives together.'

Felicitas looked worried.

'Are you afraid, little sister?' asked Perpetua.

'I'm afraid of only one thing,' Felicitas explained. 'My baby is due in about a month from now and you know what the law says, a woman who is going to have a baby should not be put in the arena. So I'm afraid that you'll all go in the arena and be taken home to heaven, and I'll be left here in prison until I have my baby then be thrown to the wild animals along with criminals rather than Christians.'

Perpetua could understand how her friend felt, and the two of them prayed about it. Their prayers were answered when Felicitas had her baby early. A member of the Christian church in Carthage took the child home to bring her up as her own.

'Let's tell each other Bible stories,' one of the young men suggested.

'Who'll start?' asked Perpetua; then she nodded to Felicitas. 'You go first.'

The slave had no doubt what she would share with her friends.

'I love the Revelation of John,' she said. 'His vision of heaven makes me want to go there.'

The others looked at her, knowing that they would indeed soon be in heaven if things didn't change dramatically for them.

'What part do you like especially?' Perpetua enquired.

Felicitas smiled, as she quoted the words, God 'will wipe every tear from their eyes. There will be no more death or mourning or crying or pain, for the old order of things has passed away.'

'Amen,' said the others together.

And the word 'amen' means 'so let it be'.

The day soon came when the young people were to die. The men were scheduled to be killed by wild beasts in the arena, all for the enjoyment of those people of Carthage who had paid to watch the spectacle. But the boar turned on its keeper and the bear refused to leave its cage. The captive leopard, which was hungry and desperate for food, pounced on one of the young men and fatally injured him.

Then it was the turn of Perpetua and Felicitas.

'Put these on,' the guard ordered, handing them clothes such as were worn by the priestesses of Ceres, robes like the ones Perpetua had dressed up in as a child.

'We cannot wear these,' Felicitas said quietly. 'We do not worship Ceres; we worship the Lord God.'

Angered by their refusal, the guards were about to take the women's robes off and send them into the arena wearing only thin underskirts. But although the crowds thought there was nothing wrong with watching Christians fed to ferocious beasts, they wouldn't have approved of them being seen in public in underskirts! So the two young women were dressed decently when they were led in to meet a fierce and hungry wild bull. Perpetua was led to the front.

'Keep on believing,' she said to her friend, and then faced the beast that was racing towards her.

The bull, foaming at the mouth from the teasing it had endured to make it angry, charged at the young woman, catching her just below the waist, and threw her to the ground. Perpetua, seeing her tunic torn, covered herself to be decent. Again the bull charged, and again she was thrown. As she struggled to her feet she saw her friend was also wounded. Raising her hand to encourage Felicitas, Perpetua slumped to the ground.

The crowd decided it was time for a break, and the beast was caught and led away. But the break was only to give a little variety to the onlookers; it was not for the good of the prisoners. Rather than bore the paying public with too many animal displays, the guards brought out their Christian prisoners, stood them where they could best be seen by the audience and prepared to put them to death by the sword.

'Slay them!' the guard yelled to the young executioner.

Raising his sword he ran it through Felicitas and the young men, but he bungled killing Perpetua. Looking him straight in the eye, she grasped the point of the sword and held it to her throat.

'Kill her!' the crowd screamed in excitement. 'Kill her!'

And he did.

Around 200 years after Perpetua, Felicitas and their friends gave their lives rather than deny their Lord, one of the most famous teachers in all of Christian history became a bishop in North Africa. His name was Augustine, and he wrote books that are still being read today, 1600 years later! He knew the story of the two women very well, and he pointed out to his students how well named Perpetua and Felicitas were. 'If you put their names together, Perpetua Felicitas, and translate the words they mean Everlasting Happiness, which is what they are now enjoying in heaven.

Fact file

 The Roman Arena: Violent spectacles were a big part of Roman entertainment. The Colosseum in Rome was used to host many gladiatorial contests where participants were forced to fight each other as well as wild beasts. The fights were usually to the death, although the crowd could cry for mercy on a gladiator they approved of. Occasionally important people chose to fight as gladiators, most famously the Emperor Commodus. Those convicted of crimes could be forced to fight in the arena or they were simply thrown to the lions in public, as many Christians were. While the Colosseum was the centre for such activity, most Roman cities had an amphitheatre for the purpose.

 Keynote: Perpetua had a very privileged upbringing and many around her would have thought that Christianity was beneath her, because most Christians at the time were slaves. She loved Jesus so much that she was willing to associate, and even die, with other Christians. She realised that her social status was helpful in this life but that it would not impress God when it came to dealing with her sin.

 Think: Perpetua and her friends encouraged themselves by remembering bits from the Bible when they were facing execution. The Bible contains many passages and stories which can help us when we are afraid. Can you think of any of them? Which would you remember in a situation like Perpetua's?

 Prayer: Lord Jesus, please help me to remember that I will never be above needing your forgiveness, and give me the strength not to deny you under pressure. Amen

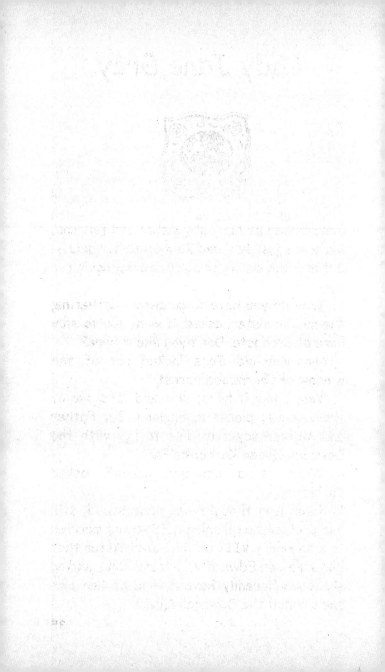

Lady Jane Grey

Jane looked at her baby sister and felt sad. Mary was just two, and Jane loved her dearly. But now she wasn't going to see her again for ages.

'Why do you have to go away?' Catherine, the middle sister, asked. 'I want you to stay here at Bradgate. Don't you like it here?'

Nine-year-old Jane looked out of the window at Charnwood Forest.

'Yes, I like it here,' she said. 'It's one of the loveliest places in England. But Father and Mother say that I've to live with the Dowager Queen Katherine Parr.'

'What is a dowager queen?' asked Catherine.

Jane, who thought she understood, still had problems explaining it. 'She was married to King Henry VIII until he died. After that her step-son Edward VI became king, and as she doesn't really have a title of her own she's called the Dowager Queen.'

'If she is a widow and is finished being a queen, does that mean that Katherine Parr is very old? '

Jane ruffled her little sister's hair.

'No, she's not very old at all. She was much younger that King Henry VIII.'

Noticing a tear beginning to run down Catherine's cheek, Jane gave her a hug.

'I don't want you to go,' the seven-year-old said. 'I want you to stay here with us.'

Later that afternoon, Jane stood at the nursery window and watched the hunt come home. Her parents had been hunting with friends, and they made a great deal of noise when they returned. Taking a seat at the window, where she couldn't be seen from outside, she listened to what the adults were saying.

'Come and see my hawks,' her father said.

'This is the best hunter I've ridden,' commented her mother, and Jane could picture the elegant Lady Frances patting her horse's rump.

'We'll meet in the games room after dinner,' suggested another voice.

'Cards it is!' laughed Lady Frances. 'A good hand of cards and a fine flagon of wine. What could be better!'

Having listened to the returning adults, Jane's mind was in a spin.

'I won't be sorry to leave Father and Mother,' she thought. 'They are so loud and they don't like me anyway. But I'll miss Catherine and Mary a lot.'

So it was that in 1547 Jane, aged just nine, left her family and moved into the home of the 'retired queen'. Her father took her to her new home in a fine carriage drawn by two of his best horses.

'Are we very rich?' Jane asked her father, when they passed poor people walking.

Henry Grey looked down at his daughter and thought she was a foolish thing.

'Of course we're rich!' he said. 'Do you think the Dowager Queen would want a poor child in her household?'

'Why does she want me there?' enquired Jane.

The Marquis of Dorset (that was her father) growled into his beard. 'Because you've got to learn to be queen just in case.'

Jane thought she'd misheard, but didn't have the courage to ask him to repeat himself.

'Are you missing home?' Queen Katherine asked Jane, a month after she arrived.

The child frowned as she thought, then she grinned.

'No, ma'am,' she said. 'I miss my little sisters, but I don't miss home at all.'

'And are you happy here?'

Jane's freckled face broke into a wide grin.

'I'm happier than I've ever been in my life before!' she said.

'Why is that?' she was asked.

'This is a happy place,' the child said. 'And you don't mind children taking part in things.'

Queen Katherine was puzzled. 'What do you mean?' she enquired.

'At home we weren't allowed to talk with adults,' Jane explained. 'And they didn't want to know what we think.'

'Well I do like to know what you think,' the handsome lady said. 'And I also like to know what you believe.'

Jane's face lit up. 'Ma'am, I believe what you do. I've heard you speaking, and I believe that the Lord Jesus Christ is my Saviour.'

Delighted with the child, Queen Katherine sat down beside her and asked about her faith.

'Tell me, Jane, what exactly you do believe.'

Without any hesitation, the child began. 'I believe that our Lord came to save us from our sins, and that we have to put our faith in him. I pray to the Lord and confess my sins every day, Ma'am.'

'And don't you need a priest to do that?' asked Queen Katherine.

'Oh no, Ma'am,' Jane said seriously, 'I can speak to God through the Lord Jesus.'

'And what about the Mass,' the older woman asked quietly. 'What do you think about the Mass?'

Jane knew the answer. She certainly did know what she believed. 'I don't believe in the Mass,' she said. 'I don't believe that the bread and wine actually become the body and blood of Jesus. They are just pictures to help us understand that the Lord Jesus died for us on the cross.'

Queen Katherine put her arm round her young friend. 'Jane Grey,' she said, 'you are a fine little Protestant. Where did you learn it all?'

'Ma'am,' said the girl shyly, 'I listened to what you and the others were saying, and learned how much you loved Christ. That made me want to know more, so I kept listening until I knew enough to believe for myself.'

'God bless you, my child,' said Queen Katherine, rising to go, 'and I'll pray for you.'

In September 1548 a terrible thing happened. Queen Katherine, who had married again, died a few days after her baby daughter was born. Jane was sent home to her parents, and she went with a broken heart. Although it was good to see her sisters again the months that followed were very unhappy. Jane wrote about them in her journal.

'When I am in the presence of Father or Mother, whether I speak, keep silent, sit, stand or go, eat, drink, be merry or sad, be sewing, playing, dancing, or doing anything else, I must do it as it were in such weight, measure and number, even so perfectly as God made the world; or I am sharply taunted and cruelly treated, sometimes with pinches, nips, and bobs and in other ways.' The only real happiness Jane found was when she was with her tutor, Mr Aylmer. 'He teaches me so gently, so pleasantly ... and when I am called from him, I fall on weeping because whatsoever else I do but learning is full of grief, trouble and fear.'

Jane was not a happy girl.

To understand what happened to Jane a few years later needs 100 words of history. When King Henry VIII died, he wanted Jane to be queen if his children had no children. His son Edward VI and his younger daughter, Elizabeth, were Protestants. His older daughter, Mary, was a Roman Catholic. The most powerful man in England, Dudley, married his son Guildford to Jane, who didn't love him. Edward died young and childless, and Dudley took Jane to the Tower of London and pronounced her queen. Dudley gave her the crown and said he'd have one made for his son. Jane realised what he was up to and announced his son would never be king. Phew! That was exactly 100 words!

'Lord, if it's your will that I am to be queen,' Jane prayed, 'then I will trust you to help me govern England for your glory.'

Jane knew she needed all the help she could get, for she was only 16 years old!

'Look at the Queen!' a boy shouted, as she journeyed down the river Thames on a barge on 10th July 1553.

'She's very tiny and thin,' someone said. 'And what red hair she has!'

'She's even shorter than she looks,' a girl pointed out, 'for she's wearing cork soled shoes to make her look taller!'

But although some people did stop to look at the new young queen, most didn't think she was queen at all! They thought that Edward VI's sister Mary should be queen, not her cousin Jane Grey.

Jane, having an interest in fashion, prepared to dress like a queen.

'Call the Master of the Wardrobe,' she told her maid.

When he arrived, he discovered that the Queen had a shopping list.

'I'll need twenty yards of velvet for dresses,' she told him, 'and plenty of fine linen cloth from Holland. Remember to order lining material for my dresses too.'

And when he went away, she began to think about the royal jewels. Having discovered what had belonged to Henry VIII, she arranged to have a strange collection of things delivered to her: some royal jewels, a collection of fish-shaped toothpicks, and the late king's shaving materials!

While Jane was busy about these things, her father-in-law had war on his mind.

'Mary is going to put up a fight for the throne,' he told Jane's father. 'I'm appointing you in charge of an army to fight against her.'

'There is no way Father is marching against Mary's army!' Jane told Dudley, when she heard the news. She knew very well what he was up to. If her father was killed, she would be completely under her father-in-law's control, and she certainly didn't want that to happen.

'You leave me no choice but to march with the army myself,' Dudley told Jane, still hoping she would change her mind.

She did not.

Dudley set out at the head of his army, but as they marched he heard of one town after another siding with Mary. Even his own army couldn't agree who should be queen. England was in a mess, and it could easily have exploded into a bloodbath. But just nine days after Jane was proclaimed queen, she found herself a prisoner under the new Queen Mary of England. Her father, who broke the news to Jane, left London and promptly became a Roman Catholic in order to keep in with the new queen, in order to keep his head firmly attached to his shoulders.

'Your Majesty, you must do something about the traitors who tried to prevent you becoming queen,' the royal advisors told Mary.

'If you mean Jane Grey, I think all she is guilty of is being young and being manipulated by powerful politicians like Dudley,' the Queen replied.

'And what will you do with Dudley?' they insisted.

Queen Mary was unwilling to have Jane beheaded, but Dudley was a different matter altogether. He was sentenced to death and executed, even though he became a Roman Catholic at the very last minute.

Jane Grey, who was still imprisoned in the Tower of London, had a staff of four.

'I don't know what I'd do without you,' she told them, 'especially you, Ellen.'

Ellen had been her nurse and lifelong companion.

'I'm glad Queen Mary is prepared to pay you to look after me until she decides on my future.'

She did not have to wait long. In mid-September Mary gave in to pressure and ordered that Jane, her husband and his three brothers, all of them Protestants, should stand trial.

Two months later, that's just what happened.

'Look at that!' a child said, who was passing the Tower of London as Jane was led out to her trial. 'What's happening?'

His mother explained. 'Lady Jane Grey is being taken to court. The man in front with the axe is the executioner, and if she is found guilty she'll be marched back with the blade of the axe facing her.'

'She looks dressed for her own funeral,' the woman standing next to her said. 'She's all in black, and she's carrying her prayer book.'

'Let's wait to see what happens,' the boy said.

They waited, and when she arrived back at the Tower the blade of the axe faced Jane.

'Does that mean she's going to have her head chopped off?' asked the child.

'It does,' his mother explained. 'And she's no more than a child herself.'

Over and again Queen Mary sent priests to the Tower of London to try to persuade her cousin Jane to become a Roman Catholic.

'I'll spare her life, if she gives up the Protestant religion,' she said. 'She doesn't need to die.'

'I can't give up the Lord I love, the Lord Jesus who died for me. If I need to, I'll die for him,' Jane told Ellen.

Wiping a tear from her eye, Ellen realised that's exactly what was going to happen.

'I've come to give you one last chance to change your mind,' the Queen's priest said, as he entered Jane's sitting-room on a cold winter morning in February 1554.

'I will not deny my Lord,' Jane said firmly. 'But I thank you for your kindness.'

Before he left, Jane asked the priest to accompany her to her execution, and prayed that God would show him the truths of the Protestant faith.

'Help me to prepare,' the teenaged Jane asked Ellen.

'I'll do everything I can for you,' her old nursemaid assured her.

Between them they chose what dress Jane would wear to her death, what she would say before she was beheaded, and where she would be buried. Ellen watched as she wrote her last letters, one to her sister and one to her father. Because Jane was a member of the royal family a small number of people were invited to see her beheaded. Among her last words she thanked the Queen's priest for his kindness. Then she knelt, in the faith that within minutes she would meet the King of Kings.

Fact file:

The Tower of London: Jane was not the first important person to be imprisoned in the Tower of London. It was used as a prison for Sir Thomas More, who did not think that Henry VIII should be the head of the Church of England, and for Anne Boleyn and Catherine Howard, two of Henry's wives. Later, it was used to imprison Sir Walter Raleigh. The Tower wasn't always a prison though. William the Conqueror built the first part as a fortress to frighten the inhabitants of London and secure his control of the city. The word 'Jane' is inscribed on the wall of one of the rooms in the Tower.

Keynote: Many people in the past have sought to use religion to gain political power, but Jane took a very different attitude. She was willing to become Queen if that was what God wanted for her, but she did not grasp power. Far from giving up what she believed to secure power, she even refused to deny Jesus to save her own life. In doing this, she showed that she realised that what was really important was a right relationship with God, not any power or authority in this world.

Think: Jane learned what she needed to know to believe in Jesus by listening carefully to the Dowager Queen and her friends when they talked of their love for the Saviour. Think about the chances that you have to listen to people talking about Jesus. Do you always make the most of them? How do you think that you could?

Prayer: Lord Jesus, you are the King of Kings and you are far more important than anyone in this world. Please help me to remember that, and not to let the things of this world distract me from following you as I should. Help me to do whatever you want me to do in this life. Amen.

Anne Askew

The two young teenagers sat on either side of the window seat and looked out over the green fields of Lincolnshire.

'This is the best place to sit when you're sewing,' Anne said. 'These tiny stitches make my head ache if I sew by candlelight.'

Her older sister smiled. 'So it's nothing to do with the view from the window?' she teased. 'And nothing at all to do with Father's groom, the young fair-haired one who looks up to the window every time he passes.'

Anne's blush began in the lower half of her neck, then it climbed slowly upwards. She willed her face not to turn red, but nothing she could do stopped the most delightful blush covering her entire face. Knowing how she looked, the girl didn't raise her eyes from her sewing, and certainly didn't look at her sister. And remembering what it was like to be thirteen, her sister didn't mention it either. Both girls continued with their embroidery in silence until well after Anne's face had returned to normal.

The morning passed pleasantly with the sisters chatting together as they sewed. And when lunchtime came they packed away their material and threads in preparation for lessons in the afternoon.

'I think we're very fortunate,' Anne said, as they climbed the stairs to the schoolroom. 'Not many girls around here are educated.'

Her sister agreed. 'Of course, it's only because Father can afford to pay for a tutor.'

Anne thought of her father and laughed. 'If Sir William Askew, Knight of Lincolnshire, can't educate his daughters, who can?'

Their tutor heard the tail end of the conversation and suggested that they make the most of the time and study one of the gospels.

Delighted with the suggestion, Anne sat down in the happy anticipation of a fascinating story about Jesus. If there was one thing their tutor could do well it was tell a story. And the ones he told best of all were from the gospels.

'I want you to imagine the River Witham,' the tutor said.

That wasn't a problem as it ran near the girls' home.

'Now,' the man went on, 'I want you to imagine many rivers joined together side by side to make a sea.'

Anne smiled. Her tutor always described the sea in the same way. Even though Anne had never seen the sea she felt it must be much more dramatic than several times the river Witham.

'Now, the story I'm going to tell you today happened on the Sea of Galilee, when the Lord Jesus and his friends went out in a boat. It was lovely when they set out, but a sudden storm blew up and the boat was in danger of sinking.'

'Sometimes boats sink in the Witham,' Anne said, 'especially in the spring floods.'

'Quite so,' agreed the tutor. 'Jesus' friends were terrified, especially as the Lord was sound asleep in the stern of the boat and making no effort to help them at all.'

Anne, who knew the story well, could picture it all.

'Eventually the men woke the Lord and accused him of not caring if they drowned! Can you remember what happened then?'

Smiling, the older girl completed the story.

'Jesus stood up and told the wind to stop. It did, and the waves became calm too.'

'And why did that happen?' their tutor asked.

Both girls, having been very well taught, answered at once, 'It happened because

51

Jesus, who made the wind and the sea, has the power to make them do what he wants them to do.'

Pleased with his pupils, the man told them they could have another gospel story if they liked. And, seeing their smiling faces, he embarked on the story of Jesus calling the fishermen to be his disciples.

'I want you to imagine many rivers joined together side by side to make a .....' be began, then caught sight of the girls' grinning faces and laughed.

Within a very few years everything changed in the Askew household. Anne's sister was thought to be old enough for marriage, and that seemed to be the most common topic of conversation in their home.

'Will you marry someone tall, dark and handsome?' Anne asked, as they sat in their favourite window seat sewing. 'Or will your husband be someone like the groom out there, stocky and fair-haired?'

'I've no idea,' the older girl replied, 'and there's not much point in me even thinking about it. Father will choose my husband and I'll not have any say in the matter.'

'I know that,' agreed Anne. 'But that doesn't stop you dreaming, does it?'

Her sister admitted that she did have her dreams. And putting down her sewing, she dreamt aloud.

'What I'd really like is a kind and considerate husband. It doesn't matter whether he's dark or fair, but he would have soft kind eyes. He'd be a good horseman, and he'd have to like children too because I want to have a big happy family.'

'Do you think I'll make a good aunt?' asked Anne.

Looking at the clever and good-natured teenager, her sister assured her that she would.

Sir William Askew did have thoughts on who would be a suitable husband for his elder daughter, and as soon as he felt she was old enough he introduced Mr Thomas Kyme to the household.

'Kyme's a very suitable match,' Sir William told his wife. 'He's wealthy enough, has land of his own, and seems to be strong and in good health.'

'Will he be a loving husband?' Mrs Askew asked.

'Loving!' spat Sir William. 'You women are all the same. Loving! Would you like her loved and poor? I tell you this,' he went on, 'if she doesn't love Kyme when she marries him then she'd better learn to love him afterwards, because my mind's made up.'

Mrs Askew knew better than make any comment, but she did want her older daughter to have a happy marriage.

Sir William's plans were finalised and arrangements made. But before the wedding could take place the young bride-to-be fell ill and did not recover. Instead of celebrating her older sister's marriage, Anne broke her heart when she attended her funeral.

'I'm determined to have Thomas Kyme as a son-in-law,' Sir William announced to his wife, not long afterwards. 'And that being the case I've offered him Anne.'

'Anne?' his wife said. 'But she's not ready to be married.'

'She had better be,' her husband said firmly, 'because Kyme is, and he's agreed to take her as his wife.'

As soon as she possibly could, Mrs Askew rushed to Anne's room to tell her what was proposed. But she was not quick enough, as she knew from the sobbing she heard when she opened her door. Without a word she put her arms round her daughter and they wept together.

'I don't want to marry Mr Kyme,' Anne said, when she had pulled herself together. 'I don't love him. Why won't Father listen to me?'

Knowing that she could never change Sir William's mind, Mrs Askew told Anne what she hoped would be true.

'You'll grow to love him,' she said. 'Give yourself time and you'll grow to love him.'

As soon as her mother left the room, Anne knelt beside her bed and prayed to the One she loved more than anyone else at all.

'Heavenly Father, if I have to marry Mr Thomas Kyme,' she prayed, 'please help me to be a good wife.'

Anne took over the Kyme household, but in fact she spent much of her time reading the Bible. And the more she studied the more perplexed she became.

'I can't find anywhere that teaches that the bread and wine become the body and blood of the Lord at the Mass,' she told one of the priests who visited her home. 'And I've read right through the whole Bible and can't find a word about Purgatory in it anywhere. Where does the Roman Church find its teaching on these things?'

'You should leave these things to bishops and priests,' the man told her. 'Don't worry your head about them. The Church will tell you what to believe.'

But Anne's tutor had done a good job. He had trained her enquiring mind to ask questions and seek answers; and that was what she did.

'I'm more than confused,' the young woman told the priest one day. 'It seems to me that the Roman Church believes more in human tradition than in the Word of God.'

'But what's wrong with that?' the man asked. 'Church traditions are just as important as the Bible. In fact, my advice to you is to stop reading the Bible and just listen to what I tell you.'

55

But that was one piece of advice that Anne's faith and conscience would not allow her to take.

'Your wife is a heretic!' the priest told Thomas Kyme, when he lost patience with the young woman. 'I've reasoned with her. I've told her what to believe. I've even threatened her, but nothing will make her change her mind.'

'What are you saying?' Kyme demanded. 'Speak clearly man!'

The priest took a deep breath. 'I'm saying that your wife is a Protestant!'

Kyme sat down heavily.

'Are you sure?' he asked.

'I know,' the priest said. 'I know she is.'

As far as Kyme was concerned that was unforgivable, and before Anne had time to make plans for her future she was put out of her home with no money to support her, and left to fend for herself. Knowing that her husband had overstepped the mark, she headed for London to try to sort things out through the authorities there. But her reputation as a Protestant went before her.

'You are arrested on the charge of being a Protestant,' Anne was told in March 1545, not long after she arrived in London. 'And you will stand trial at the Saddlers' Hall.'

'Do you have anything to say?' she was asked.

'No sir,' Anne replied. 'I will keep all I have to say until my trial. That way it cannot be twisted into what I've never said at all.'

When the day of her trial arrived, questions were thrown at her thick and fast.

'Do you admit that you said you'd rather read five lines in the Bible than hear five Masses said?' the prosecutor asked.

'I did say that,' Anne agreed. 'Five verses of the Bible do my soul good where five Masses do not.'

The faces of those in the Saddlers' Hall lost their sympathetic look. Anne might be a woman, but she still seemed to be a heretic.

'The prisoner certainly knows what she believes,' a man said to the person sitting next to him. 'Even if it's a lot of Anti-Romanist propaganda.'

It was a long trial, but Anne was eventually discharged into the safekeeping of some friends, provided she remained with them in case she was recalled to the court.

Less than a year passed then she was again summoned to appear before the Council.

'The charge,' announced the prosecutor, 'is that the prisoner refuses to believe that the bread and wine of the Mass are the actual body and blood of the Lord.'

For five hours Anne was questioned, and for five hours she stood firm in her belief that the Bible is the Word of God, and the basis for faith rather than the teaching and traditions of the Roman Church.

'Remand the prisoner until tomorrow when the case against her will be continued,' ruled the exhausted judge, at the end of two days of questioning.

The following day, although Anne Askew was very unwell, she was taken before Sir Richard Rich, who did all he could to make her give up her Protestant faith. When he totally failed to do that, he had her sent to the Tower of London to be racked. Anne was laid on the rack and her arms and legs were stretched until they were almost out of their sockets. In fact, her legs may have been pulled out of their sockets, as she was unable to walk again. Anne held true to her faith despite all that was done to her.

'If you become a Roman Catholic you'll be safe and well looked after,' the Lord Chancellor told her. 'But if you don't, you'll be sent out and burned.'

Anne held firm.

On 16th July 1546, an enormous crowd gathered at Smithfield Market in London to watch the burning at the stake of four heretics, one of them a woman. The three men walked to the unlit fire that was prepared for them. Anne, who was crippled following being on the rack, was carried there in a chair.

'What are they doing to her?' a woman asked her husband.

'They're chaining her chair to the stake,' he explained.

After all four Christians were secured to their stakes a priest preached a terrible sermon to them. When he'd finished speaking, the four prayed together.

'Take it to them,' said the Lord Chancellor, after the prayer.

His servant walked over to the four Protestants with a piece of paper saying that if they agreed to give up their Bible beliefs the King would pardon them.

Anne refused even to look at the paper, and the three men were equally courageous.

'Let justice be done!' the Lord Mayor shouted.

Raising a blazing torch in the air, the executioner walked towards the prisoners and set light to the fire, so making them martyrs. Anne Askew and her three companions gave up their lives rather than deny the Lord Jesus, and the fires were still burning when they were welcomed home to heaven.

Fact file:

 Lincolnshire: The county where Anne lived is on the east coast of England and, although she had never seen the sea, part of the county where she lived was once under water. A large area was drained and reclaimed by a Dutch engineer called Cornelius Vermuyden in the 17th century, so Lincolnshire is larger now than it was in Anne's day. The Witham is one of three rivers in Lincolnshire and, while it may flood at the spring tide, the Trent can have a wave over 1m high on it at the same tide.

 Keynote: Anne did not want to marry Mr Thomas Kyme, but she had no option because of the social conditions of her day. In that situation, she humbly submitted to God and asked that he would help her to be a good wife. We may find ourselves in situations that we would have preferred to avoid, but even there we must seek to glorify God and do our job as well as we can.

Think: Anne was able to see that the things the priest was telling her were wrong, because she had learned to look at the Bible for herself and to think about what it said. If she had not done so, she would not have known any better than to believe the wrong things that she was being told. What can you do to learn to read the Bible for yourself so that you can do the same thing?

 Prayer: Lord Jesus, thank you for giving us the Bible so that we can understand the difference between truth and lies. Please help me to be faithful to your Word in every situation. Amen.

Lysken Dirks

Lysken slipped her feet into her new clogs and clopped across the stone floor of her home. Then she did a little tap-dance that made her father smile.

'Are they the right size?' Mr Dirks asked.

'Yes, Papa,' the child grinned. 'They're the right size, the right shape and just the right sound. I love the clopping of new clogs.'

Tap dancing to her mother, who was sitting on a low seat by the fire feeding the newest member of the family, the child clipped to a standstill in front of her, then did a twirl that made the baby smile.

'May I go with you to the market tomorrow?' she asked.

Mrs Dirks laughed. 'Would this sudden interest in going to the market have anything to do with clip clopping along the street like a newly-shod pony?'

The eight-year-old smiled. 'I'll not be sure that they're quite right for walking in the town unless I try,' she said. 'And tomorrow

63

is your vegetable day, and I could help you to carry them home.'

'Indeed you could,' her father said. 'And I think that's a very good idea too. You're growing into a big girl and Mama could certainly use your help.'

To get to the market, Mrs Dirks and Lysken had to walk quite a long distance. But it was a sunny January day, just right for trying out new clogs, and Grandmother Dirks was looking after the baby.

'Let's go by the Vlaaykensgang,' suggested Mrs Dirks. 'You'd like that.'

Forgetting all about her new clogs, Lysken ran at her mother's side. 'Is that where the bell-ringers play, and where all the shoemakers work?'

'Yes,' the woman agreed. 'It's one of the shortest streets in Antwerp, but one of the most interesting.'

'Tell me about it,' said Lysken, as they wove through the narrow town streets.

'In the evenings amateur musicians gather in the Vlaaykensgang, great numbers of bell-ringers among them. Then, when the bell in the cathedral tower begins to ring, they all join in and make wonderful tunes together. It fills the whole night sky with sound.'

'We only hear them at home when the wind's in the right direction,' the girl pointed out. 'May I come to hear them one night?'

Mrs Dirks smiled. 'When you're older you can,' she said.

'Older seems such a long time away,' Lysken said. 'But I suppose it will come one day.'

Just then they reached the right corner and turned into the Vlaaykensgang. The tap tapping of hammers drowned out the clopping of Lysken's clogs.

'That's like music too,' the girl said.

'So it is,' laughed Mrs Dirks. 'But that's the music of shoemakers hammering soles on leather shoes.'

The pair wandered the length of the Vlaaykensgang, looking at one shoemaker after another. Some worked on clogs, but others made shoes out of fine leather.

'Will I ever have leather shoes like those ones?' asked the child.

'You would have to marry a very rich man to wear leather shoes,' Mrs Dirks pointed out. 'And I think you'd rather marry a good and a happy man than a rich one.'

The girl agreed... though wearing shoes made of leather dyed red seemed a lovely idea.

From the Vlaaykensgang the pair walked to the vegetable market where they filled a sack with food for the family.

'I'll carry it,' Lysken said.

Taking the heavy sack from her mother, she swung it over her back and they set off for home. The sun was setting and the bright winter light shone in their eyes as they walked.

'It's hard to see!' laughed the girl. 'The sun is so low in the sky that it almost joins up with its reflection in the water.'

'And there's a lot of water in Antwerp!' laughed her mother. 'There are waterways all through the city, and then there is all the rain that falls.'

'Don't let's talk about the rain,' Lysken teased. 'This is the best day we've had for weeks, so let's enjoy it.'

That's just what they did as they walked along the towpath of one waterway, then along the side of another, before reaching the little street in which was their home.

Although older felt a long time away when she was eight, the years seemed to pass quickly, and in a shorter time that she had imagined, Lysken was 18.

'Would you like to walk along the waterside?' asked Jeronius Segerson. 'It's a lovely evening and we have so much to talk about.'

It's probably safer to talk as we walk,' the young woman agreed. 'It seems sometimes as though the house walls of Antwerp have ears, and we have to be so careful these days.'

Although the young couple were in love, their conversation that night was not about happy things.

'Being a Christian here is very dangerous just now,' Jeronius said. 'And being a Baptist is even more so.'

Lysken agreed.

'Do you know what the King did in Brussels some time ago?' she asked, though she didn't wait for an answer. 'They hung pictures of the reformers at the gates of the city and paid people to give them in to the authorities. The rewards were so great that many people reported their friends and neighbours for being Protestants!'

'And I don't think any of them survived,' said Jeronius sadly, 'for a law was passed before that saying that death by fire was the punishment for Baptists who would not deny their faith. If they did deny their faith they were killed by the sword. But that wasn't a choice for them, for no true believer, in Jesus Christ would deny their faith just to be run through with a sword.'

A shudder went up Lysken's back.

'Are you all right?' Jeronius asked.

Nodding, the young woman straightened her back and walked briskly along the towpath. 'Yes,' she said. 'I'm all right. But I wonder if I would be as courageous if the same were to happen to me.'

'God grant that it won't,' he said. 'I pray that it won't.'

All marriages in Holland and Flanders had to be conducted by the Roman Church. That caused a problem for Jeronius and Lysken when they decided to get married.

'We can't go to a priest to marry us,' she said.

'No,' Jeronius agreed. 'But we could be married in our own congregation and by our own minister. The state wouldn't recognise us as man and wife, but God would.'

So it was that the young couple were married in the presence of their Christian friends. Having found a humble home in Antwerp, they settled down to a quiet life, knowing that the less they were seen in public the safer they were. Sunday after Sunday they met with their friends for worship, changing the venue regularly in order not to make neighbours suspicious. Their Baptist friends were a great support to them.

In 1551 King Charles V, in a fit of rage against Protestants (especially Baptists), clamped down on those living in Antwerp and other large towns. Soon his men were seen pounding the streets on Sunday mornings searching for gatherings that might be Christians worshipping. Sometimes they rammed doors down just to discover gamblers playing cards or groups of men gathered for cockfights and dogfights. Underhand tactics were what the soldiers were best at. 'We'll help get your son out of trouble if you tell us which of your neighbours are Baptists.' 'We'll give you protection if you give us information.' And sometimes their methods were more brutal. Young people were beaten up and questioned to try to make them give information about their parents and their friends.

It was inevitable that Jeronius and Lysken would come to the notice of the King's men eventually, especially as none of their neighbours could remember them being married in the Roman Church.

'They're not married at all,' the gossip next door said. 'They're just living together.'

'You don't say!' whispered her neighbour, rushing off to pass on the news to all her friends.

'Maybe they are brother and sister,' suggested a kindly lady down the road. 'Perhaps their parents are dead and they look after each other.'

But the gossip soon scotched that suggestion. 'Have you not noticed,' she said, 'that young woman who calls herself Mrs Segerson looks to me as if she's going to have a baby?'

Tongues wagged their way right along the street, and down all the side streets too. Whether or not that's how the King's men found out they were Christians doesn't really matter, what matters is that the young couple were arrested within a year of being married, and before their baby was born. They were thrown into separate cells in the prison and never saw each other again.

Lysken and Jeronius were not able to speak to each other, but they were able to write. For some reason they were allowed pens, ink and paper in their cells. Perhaps the soldiers expected them to write things that would incriminate them, or perhaps they hoped they would mention the names of other Christians in their letters, so allowing them to be arrested too. If that's why the prison guards allowed the young couple to write to each other they must have been very disappointed.

'Let's see what he's written this time!' growled the guard on duty to the one who was just going off.

Unfolding the sheet of paper the man looked at it and spat.

'Poetry!' he gasped. 'You would think when they were going to be killed they'd write something more interesting that poetry!'

The other guard took the page and read it aloud.

> *Fear God always,*
> *In loathsome cell,*
> *guarded and strong, I lie*
> *Bound in Christ's love,*
> *his truth to testify.*

Though wall be thick,
  no hand the doors unclose,
  God is my strength,
  my solace, and repose.

Then the two men burst out laughing, truly horrible laughs.

'So he thinks his cell is loathsome, does he?' one said. 'Let's see how much worse we can make it for him.'

The other rubbed his hands at the thought. 'I wonder if he'll feel bound in Christ's love after we've done our worst!'

But whatever was done to them, the two young people held fast to their faith, and trusted in Jesus to care for them.

After their trial, at which Lysken was judged to be 'the greatest heretic in town', Jeronius wrote a letter to encourage his young wife.

'My most beloved wife, submit yourself to all that is happening to you; be patient in all your troubles; keep praying, and focus your mind on the precious promises God has made to those who trust in him to the end.'

Lysken's reply was equally moving. 'My most dearly beloved husband in the Lord, ... If we suffer for Jesus we shall also reign with him. I leave you in God's hands ... The grace of the Lord be with us.'

When offered the opportunity to deny his faith and avoid being burned at the stake, Jeronius stood firm. Lysken had an even harder time than he did, because the court tried to tempt her to abandon her faith in Jesus for the sake of her unborn baby. At the time she stood upright and brave, but on returning to her prison cell the young woman wept in anguish.

'Don't worry about our baby,' Jeronius wrote, when he heard how she was. 'Our friends will care for it. The Lord will watch over it.'

With the love of her husband whom she could not see, and the prayer support of her Christian friends, Lysken struggled through that terrible time and once again found peace in her Lord.

In September 1551, Jeronius was burnt at the stake, one of over 400 Protestants who lost their lives in Holland and Flanders because they believed that the truths of the Bible were worth dying for. Lysken's case was longer coming to its conclusion, though in the end the authorities rushed events to prevent a scene.

'On Saturday morning we rose early, some time before day,' wrote someone who was in Antwerp at the time,' but the crafty murderers were quicker that we were. While we slept they finished their murderous work

72

between 3 and 4 in the morning. Taking Lysken from her prison cell they put her in a sack and drowned her before we arrived. A few people were there and told us that she went to her death courageously. Her last words, on behalf of her baby and herself were, "Father, into your hands I commend my spirit."'

Secretly, and in just ones and twos, her friends visited the place over the next few days.

'We often walked along the waterways of Antwerp,' one said. 'And as we walked we talked of Jesus and all he had done for us. Sometimes we spoke of heaven, and now Jeronius and Lysken are there with the Lord.'

'Why do I feel so sad when I know they are now so happy?' her friend asked.

They stood in silence for a minute or two, watching the reflection of the setting sun on the water where Lysken had drowned.

'We're sad because we'll miss them. But Jesus remembers what it's like to lose a friend, and he understands.'

Turning from the terrible scene, they set out for home with the warmth of God's sun shining down on them.

Fact file:

 The Low Countries: Britain was not the only place where there were arguments between the Protestants and the Roman Church. The Low Countries were under the influence of Spain at the time. When the teaching of the Reformers began to take hold in the Low Countries, they were put down very forcefully as part of the Spanish Inquisition, during which the Roman Church and Spanish government tried to stamp out all that they regarded as heresy.

 Keynote: Lysken's neighbours gossiped about her living with someone that she was not married to, because she had not gone through a Romanist marriage service. People were misinterpreting her actions and using them to spread gossip about her. But Lysken was prepared to put up with that for the sake of what she knew was right. We cannot control what other people say about us, but we know that God knows the truth and it is his opinion that matters.

Think: Lysken and her husband loved each other very much, and it must have made both of them sad to think of the other suffering. But neither of them advised the other to give up. It can be tempting to do the wrong thing, or to suggest that someone else does the wrong thing to stop people getting hurt. In the end, however, God is in control and he wants us to do what is right.

Prayer: Lord Jesus, thank you for the people who encourage me to follow you. Please help me to encourage others to do the same, and keep me from pulling them down with gossip. Amen.

Marion Harvey

Marion and her mother walked along the shore. Because Marion was just ten years old it wasn't so far for her to bend down to the sand at her feet to gather the smaller pieces of driftwood the last tide had brought in. But for her mother it was backbreaking work, and work she did every day of the year, except Sundays. And this was Saturday.

'I hate doing this,' the girl complained. 'I want to go and play.'

'It needs done, my child,' said Mrs Harvey. 'If there's no wood for the fire, there's no food for the table. It's as simple as that.'

Rebuked, but only slightly, Marion changed tack.

'I hate gathering wood on Saturdays because we need to carry so much. Why can't we just come tomorrow and get Sunday's wood instead of doing twice as much today.'

The woman sighed deeply but quietly so that Marion didn't see how much her complaints hurt.

'Tomorrow's the Sabbath, my child,' Mrs Harvey explained yet again — because this conversation was carried on most Saturday mornings — 'and the Good Book tells us that we shouldn't work on the Sabbath. It's the day on which God rested after his work of creation, and he's given it to us as a day of rest too.'

'But it's not really a rest if it just means we've got to do twice as much the day before,' the ten-year-old insisted.

Mrs Harvey had had enough. 'It does you no credit to argue with God's Word, my child.'

Knowing that was the end of the conversation, Marion separated from her mother and gathered the driftwood more and more slowly; not feeling in the least guilty that it meant her mother would have to carry even more.

Although Marion thought she was worked hard as a child, she discovered what hard work was really like just a few years later when she became a servant girl to a wealthy family in her home village of Borrowstouness, on the shores of Scotland's Firth of Forth. (Borrowstouness is now called Bo-ness).

'I can't wait to get home for a break,' she told the other servant in the household. 'This work is killing me.'

'The mistress will kill you before the work does if you don't get on with it,' her friend replied.

Marion, who was sitting on the kitchen floor putting black polish on the stones round the open fire where all the cooking was done, rubbed so hard for a minute that it seemed she was trying to rub the whole world into the ground. Which, if the truth be told, was exactly what Marion Harvey often felt like doing.

'I spend all week slaving here and looking forward to going home for a break. Then most Saturday evenings I'm allowed home for a whole 24 hours, and what happens there? Dad spends all his time reading the Bible and going to conventicles, and I've got to sit and listen to all his readings and long prayers. When I'm here I wish I was at home, then when I get home I remember what it's like and wish I was here. What a life!'

The other maid seemed to know what her friend was thinking.

'Looking forward to Saturday?' she asked cheekily.

And she was one very lucky girl, because if the mistress of the house had not come into the kitchen at just that moment, she might have had a smear of black lead applied to her face! Marion contained her irritation until the kitchen door was safely shut with her mistress on the other side.

'It's so annoying,' she said. 'The truth is that I really respect Dad for what he believes. He's dead against the King trying to make the church in Scotland like the church in England, with bishops, a prayer book and all that. He says that's halfway to becoming Romanists again. That's why he signed the Solemn League and Covenant, and why he's forever out on the hillsides listening to illegal preachers.'

'Have you ever gone with him?' asked the other servant girl.

'Once or twice,' moaned Marion. 'These things are so important to Dad and Mum that we were taken along if they thought we'd be safe enough.'

'And was it all fire and brimstone?' giggled her friend. 'Were the preachers all old men with bad tempers and long beards full of crumbs?'

Marion sat back on her knees and laid the polish down at her side. Her face took on a dreamy kind of a look.

'Actually, it wasn't like that,' she said. 'Much of the time the men preached about the love of God. And they weren't old men, at least not all of them. There were some really nice young men among the field preachers.'

'Oh yes!' teased her friend, 'Good-looking, were they?'

Marion, whose mind was up on a hillside near Linlithgow, didn't realise she was being made a fool of.

'Some of them were,' she agreed. 'Some of them were very good-looking.'

Just then the mistress barged into the kitchen, obviously having listened from outside the door.

'Marion Harvey!' she said. 'This is neither the time nor the place to be discussing young men, good looking or not. And if you don't get on with the work you'll be discussing them elsewhere, for you'll be no servant of mine!'

Picking up the black lead, Marion rubbed like she'd never rubbed polish before.

When the door slammed shut, she found herself worrying that the mistress might have overheard about the conventicles, but decided from the row that only the discussion about good looks had been overheard.

The next Sunday set the pattern for many others to follow. Marion made it clear that although she would sit through the family Bible reading and worship, she was doing it out of politeness rather than because she was really interested. And even though it made both her parents very sad, she went out with her friends on Sundays.

'That's not how the Lord's Day should be spent,' Mr Harvey said sadly. 'It should be spent in worship and meditation on God's Word.'

'I'll leave the rest of you to do that, Father. But I'm going out with my friends.'

What Marion would have known had she thought about it at all, was that as soon as she left the house her father knelt down and poured out his sad heart to the Lord, pleading that his rebellious daughter would soon know the truth.

Marion and her friends decided to go for a walk, and set out from Borrowstouness east along the Firth of Forth to Blackness and back. As they walked they discussed all the things girls discuss. They were louder than well brought up girls of the day, and even Marion was a little taken aback by the language some of them used. It was so foreign to all she'd been brought up to accept as right. Some of her friends even used the Lord's name as a swear word! The first time Marion did that she thought the heavens might open and swallow her up, but they didn't. And somehow it became easier to do the more she did it. By the time they were half-way home from Blackness, Marion was beginning to feel quite at home with how she was speaking.

'Watch it!' she said to herself, as she entered the door of her parents' house. 'If I do that here, Dad will die of heart failure.'

Not many years passed till one day Marion Harvey decided to go along to a conventicle. Perhaps one of the good-looking young men was to be the preacher, or perhaps curiosity just got the better of her. She told the other maid in the household what she was going to do.

'Don't be a fool!' her friend said. 'You know what'll happen if you're caught.'

'I'll not be caught,' said Marion. 'Most of the meetings are in hollows between the hills, and the worshippers post lookouts on all the hills round about. Any sign of the King's troops and there's a warning whistle that sends everyone heading off in all directions. The most the soldiers would find when they reached the meeting place would be some downtrodden grass.'

Marion did go to the field meeting, and she went back again and again. Perhaps her friend noticed the change in her first, when she stopped swearing and began talking about people in a much kinder and gentler way. Or it may be that her parents were first to see the beginnings of answered prayer when their daughter came home on Saturday evenings and didn't look irritated when her father took the Bible down from the shelf, or sigh with boredom several times during his prayer. Whoever noticed it first doesn't matter, because before long her family and friends knew for sure that Marion had changed. Her eyes shone, her language was pure and she seemed to love the family times of worship. Not only that, she was first to have her shawl round her shoulders when her father was getting ready to go to the field meetings on Sundays.

'Where are you heading tomorrow to hear your blood and thunder preaching?' her fellow servant asked, one day in 1680. 'Is it off to hear that fanatic Mr Donald Cargill?'

Marion refused to let her friend annoy her.

'It is,' she replied. 'And a man less given to preaching blood and thunder would be hard to find. Mr Cargill preaches about the love of God so beautifully that I not only know I love the Saviour, I feel IN love with him. And there's nothing more beautiful than that.'

Seeing the scorn on her friend's face, Marion tightened her jute brat (apron) around her waist and went back to work.

It was near Edinburgh that Marion was caught along with others who were walking together to a conventicle some months later. Edinburgh, which is over 20 miles from Borrowstouness, seemed not too far to go to the meeting when they wanted so much to be there. Marion, who was used to the wide-open spaces of the Firth of Forth, who loved the air blowing in her hair and the taste of sea salt on her lips, found herself locked up in prison. But although her body was incarcerated her mind could roam free. She imagined herself as one of a great crowd listening to Donald Cargill, and she could almost hear the psalm-singing echoing round a hollow in the hills. With great concentration Marion remembered what she'd heard preached and thought over the points in her mind. It was better, she thought, to think about such things than to think about the future. Although the not-so-far future was a joyous thought, and she took comfort in thinking of heaven.

The King's court had little sympathy with Covenanters like Marion, and when she was tried she found herself surrounded by clever men who aimed to confuse her. She answered as best and as truthfully as she could.

'What age are you?' she was asked.

And even that question was hard for her.

'I'm not sure.' Marion replied. Age was not much of an issue with servant girls in the 17th Century.

'Put down that she's 20,' the clerk said.

'How long is it since you saw Mr Donald Cargill?' asked the prosecutor.

'I don't know exactly,' Marion said truthfully.

'Was it within the last three months?'

'It might have been.'

'Do you hold to the Covenants that would see a Scottish Presbyterian church even though it's against the law and the wishes of the King?' the questioning went on.

'Yes,' said Marion, 'because they agree with the Bible.'

'And do you hold to the authority of the King?'

Marion answered as best she could. 'Yes, so long as the King holds the truth of God. But when he broke his oath and robbed Christ of his kingly rights we were bound to disown him.'

The questioning might as well have stopped there, though it did not, for Marion's words had condemned her.

Some months later, in January 1681, Marion went through another trial before the Lords Justiciary, she was pronounced to be guilty of treason and the sentence was given.

'Marion Harvey, you will be taken to the Grassmarket of Edinburgh on Wednesday next, between two and four o'clock in the afternoon, and there be hanged on a gibbet till you be dead, and all your possessions are to be forfeited to His Majesty's use.'

Much good Marion's possessions would have been to the King, for she was only a poor servant girl.

Marion, and another Covenanter called Isabel Alison, were to be hung together with five women guilty of child murder. And if the two Christian women were concerned about being hanged along with criminals they most likely remembered that Jesus was hung on the cross between thieves. Edinburgh's Grassmarket nestles at the foot of the great Castle Hill, and the people who came to watch the spectacle no doubt sat on the steep hillside to get a good view. What they saw was two young women walking meekly to be hanged, and what they heard was them singing a psalm before the ropes were put round their necks. What the other five women did or said is not recorded.

'That's the end of the troublemakers,' said one of the lawyers who came to watch.

'And the King's better off without them,' replied the other.

What they neither knew nor cared was that Marion Harvey and Isabel Alison had gone from their presence to be with the Kings of Kings.

Fact file:

 Going into service: Many years ago there were very few jobs available to young girls. Universities were very slow to allow girls to go there to study and poor people could not afford to go in any case. One of the few options was going to stay with a rich family and work as a servant. This often meant living a long way from home and working very hard for long hours. The government did very little to prevent employers from mistreating their servants.

 Keynote: When Marion was young, all of the things that her father did seemed very boring. But later she was willing to die for doing the same things. In between she learned that they had a value which she could not see until she came to love Jesus herself. In the end, Jesus was worth far more than anything else she could ever have. When God teaches you to love Bible reading and prayer, you will realise that they provide you with greater riches than the rest of the world can give.

Think: When Marion first began to use the Lord's name as a swear word, it really frightened her, But little by little it got easier and easier until she had to take special care not to do it in front of her father. This is the case with a lot of sins. The more we do them, the more hardened we become to them. Can you think of occasions when this has happened to you? What can you do about it?

Prayer: Lord Jesus, please help me not to be scared when people in authority try to make me disown you. Help me to remember your great promises and the blessings you have given to your people over the years. Amen.

Margaret Wilson

It had rained all day, every single minute of it. Now, just before sunset, the rain stopped and Mrs Wilson suggested that a walk would be a good idea. 'You'll not sleep tonight if you don't get a breath of fresh air into your lungs.'

Margaret was delighted with the suggestion. She'd had a really hard day looking after her sister and brother while their mother worked on the farm. Not only that, but she'd had to make butter as well.

'Can we help make the butter?' Agnes and Thomas had asked, over and over again.

Patiently Margaret had given them shots each at turning the handle on the butter churn, all the time knowing that their young arms made no difference at all to the production of butter, other than making the job last longer. And when the butter was almost on the turn, she made sure that the youngsters were there to turn the handle so that they felt they'd done the job.

'We made the butter for Margaret!' the boy and girl had said excitedly, when their mother came in from feeding the hens.

Mrs Wilson knew that entertaining her younger children was no easy job, and she was sure Margaret would enjoy a walk in the evening sun. As soon as they left Glenvernock (their father's farm) the younger children ran on in front like dogs let off a leash.

'You're good with the wee ones,' said Mrs Wilson. 'I hope you know I appreciate your help, especially on a day like this when they couldn't get out to let off steam.'

'They can be menaces,' the girl laughed. 'But they're great company really.'

And just as she said that, the 'great company' arrived back in a flurry of arms, legs and loud shouts.

'We saw someone up on the hill!' Thomas said. 'Do you think it was a thief or a robber?'

'More likely to be a shepherd,' Mrs Wilson laughed. But there was an edge to her laugh that only Margaret noticed. 'In any case,' the woman said, 'the sun's nearly down and it's time we turned for home.'

'Can't I go and see if the shepherd needs help?' pleaded Thomas, sensing an adventure in the making.

'You certainly cannot,' his mother said firmly. 'Ten-year-olds need their sleep.'

'What about seven-year-olds?' Agnes asked.

Mrs Wilson laughed. 'They need it even more!'

Margaret, who was twelve, knew she wouldn't be put to bed as soon as they arrived home. She was glad about that as there was something she wanted to ask her mother.

'That man on the hillside,' she said, as soon as the younger two were tucked up, 'do you think he was a shepherd?'

Looking at her daughter curiously, Mrs Wilson wondered what was behind the question. 'How much does the girl know?' she considered.

And the answer came back immediately.

'I thought he might have been a Covenanter,' said Margaret. 'I've heard they're often in the hills around here.'

Her mother looked anxious.

'I'm sure they are,' she said. 'And I hope tonight's little encounter was as near as you'll get to meeting any of them.'

'But what's wrong with them?' Margaret asked. 'I thought they just held church services out on the hills, and that sounds great!'

'Don't let your father hear you say that,' her mother warned. 'They may only be holding services, but they're also breaking the law. And some of them don't live to come home and tell their wives about it.'

'Why not?' the girl asked, confused by her mother's answer.

'Ask your father when he comes in if he's not too tired,' Mrs Wilson said, and Margaret knew that was her last word on the subject.

Margaret did ask her father that night, and the story he told her made the girl sad.

'Over a hundred years ago, in 1560, the church in Scotland was changed from Roman Catholic to Protestant,' he began.

'Was that a good thing?' Margaret asked.

Her father smiled. 'Yes,' he said, 'it was. The Roman Church was in a mess at the time. But don't interrupt me, because you put me off my story. Where was I? Yes, that change was called the Reformation. Mary Stuart was Queen of Scotland then. But when James became king, he wanted the Scottish church to be the same as the English church, and that became law. The men in the hills want the Scottish church to be restored, and they argue that it's more in line with what the Bible teaches. But they're breaking the law holding their meetings – they call them conventicles – and when they're caught, they're punished.'

'Are they called Covenanters because they hold conventicles?' enquired the girl.

Her father screwed up his face in thought. 'No,' he said. 'It's because they signed a covenant to show what they believe.

'Do you think they're wrong?' the teenager asked.

'Yes,' he said. 'Your mother and I are more than happy to worship the way the King wants. And you will be too.'

Over the years that followed, Margaret discovered more about the Covenanters, and she read her Bible too.

'They're right,' she decided. 'They are good and brave men and women who are standing up for what Jesus teaches.'

Several times she tried to ask her father more about the subject, but she met with a stone wall. The King was right, and that was all there was to say. But by the time she was sixteen, Margaret was quite sure in her heart that the King was wrong. Not only that, she discussed it with her brother and sister and they agreed with her.

'Should we head for the hills to join the Covenanters?' Thomas asked.

Margaret's heart said a loud 'yes', but she was in a terrible quandary. She could make that decision for herself, but could she make it for her brother and sister? Even Agnes had decided she would go if Margaret did. But in the end no decision was taken.

One day, when the Wilson children were out in the fields, a soldier barged into the farmhouse and addressed their mother, 'We've heard that your children are sympathetic to the Covenanters.'

'But they're not here,' Mrs Wilson gasped.

'Very well then,' barked the officer. 'We'll be back and then they will have to take the Abjuration Oath.'

The colour drained from Mrs Wilson's face.

'Tell me what the Abjuration Oath is,' she whispered.

The soldier cleared his throat. 'Taking the Oath shows you support the King, and that you agree with him that the church should be run by the state.'

Turning on his heel, the soldier left.

'We'll be back!' he said, as he slammed the door behind him. 'Soon!'

Although it broke their parents' hearts, the young people had no choice but to head for the hills.

'Where'll we go?' Agnes asked.

Margaret had already thought through her plan. 'We'll go inland from Wigton. And if we keep going to the headwaters of the Malzie we should get some shelter. There are trees there, and there will be plenty of fresh water.'

It was a brave trio of teenagers who tramped up the riverside, taking wide detours when they passed the house at Newmilns and the Torhouse Mill.

'There aren't any more houses are there?' Agnes asked.

'Not for a while,' Margaret assured her. 'But we've got to keep to the Malzie or we'll be lost. One hill looks just like another, and the streams look the same too.

'There are the trees!' Thomas said. 'Is that where we're heading?'

'Not quite,' said Margaret. 'That's Corsemalzie, and we'll have to detour round it, before we turn south along another stream that will take us up to Airriequhillart. We should have cover and safety there, and we might meet up with the Covenanters.'

That was just the beginning of their adventures; for Margaret, Thomas and Agnes knew that they could never return home again. They were outlaws, and their lives were in grave danger from the King's men. They moved from place to place, eating whatever they could find and sheltering in caves, under bushes and even up trees when they thought they heard soldiers. Whenever they could, the young folk attended conventicles where they heard the Bible preached faithfully. And when they could not, they talked about sermons they'd heard, and prayed together.

'It's the soldiers again!' Mrs Wilson told her husband. 'They're coming back.'

Mr Wilson shook his head. 'And they'll keep coming back till they find the children, wherever they are. They probably think we're leaving out food and clothes for them.'

His wife sobbed. 'I only wish we could.'

'We'd be shot if we tried,' Mr Wilson said, 'and we might be shot anyway.'

Few homes were more closely watched by the King's men than Glenvernock. The young folk knew they could never go back there so they steered well clear of the place. However, sometimes they managed to get news to their parents that they were safe and well.

The winter was worst.

'There are no berries left,' Agnes said, 'and no nuts.'

'God won't see us starve,' Margaret told her young sister. 'There are still fish in the rivers, and I've almost gathered enough wild things to make us some soup.'

'Do you remember our mother's broth?' asked Thomas, and then wished he had not. He could almost smell the stuff, and it made his heart ache as well as his tummy.

But that afternoon, when they arrived at the conventicle, a woman they knew gave them a wooden bowl of broth – cold, but broth. And it tasted just as good as their mother's.

'Now that you're fed you can be lookout,' Thomas was told.

He climbed the hill nearest the gathering, and then lay down behind a gorse bush to watch for soldiers. No sooner had the psalm singing begun, than Thomas saw movement in the valley below. Watching for a minute or two, he decided he was right. The boy slithered down the hillside to the meeting and gave the warning. Amazingly the 40 people who were present were able to melt into the hillside, and by the time the soldiers arrived there was nobody there to be caught.

'Someone must have tipped the soldiers off,' said Agnes. 'We're going to have to be even more careful.'

In February 1685, Margaret and Agnes decided to risk a secret visit to friends in the small town of Wigton. Thomas stayed up on the snowy hillside and awaited their return.

'Let's drink the King's health!' suggested someone in the company they were visiting.

Agnes looked at her sister, and then looked quickly away.

They didn't raise their cups to toast the King. Had anyone noticed?

Someone got up from the table and went out of the door. Margaret and Agnes realised they were going to be betrayed to the authorities.

'You're the Wilson girls!' a man they didn't recognise said. 'We've been waiting for you to come!'

There was nowhere to run. Margaret and Agnes were trapped and they couldn't even get news to their brother.

'Where are you taking us?' Margaret asked the soldier who was called to drag them away.

'You're going in the Thieves' Hole,' spat the man, who was sick to death of Covenanters, and just wanted to get home to his wife.

'But we're not thieves,' Agnes protested.

'Maybe not!' the soldier sneered. 'Maybe the Thieves' Hole is too good for the King's traitors.'

But that's where they landed, and they suffered there for seven long weeks.

Two months later, on 13th April, Margaret and Agnes stood trial, along with an old widow woman and a servant girl. All were Covenanters; all trusted in the Lord Jesus with all their hearts.

'Guilty!' the verdict was pronounced.

Margaret Wilson was sentenced to death along with the old woman, whose name was Margaret MacLachlan. Mr Wilson paid a large amount of money to have young Agnes released into his custody, and she went home to pray.

It was four weeks later, on 11th May 1685, that the sentence was carried out. Agnes knew exactly what would happen, and she prayed that the two Margarets would be brave, and that the end would come soon.

At low water the tide at Wigton goes out a very long distance, leaving acres of wet sand. When the tide comes in, it rushes up what used to be the path of a river so quickly that many people have been drowned there as they tried to reach dry land. Margaret Wilson, aged 18, and Margaret MacLauchlan, aged 63, could not run to safety for they were tied to stakes securely hammered into the sand. The older woman was put further out in order that she drowned first in full view of young Margaret. And a crowd gathered to watch it all happen.

'If they shout out that they'll take an oath to the King, run in and cut them free before it's too late,' the soldiers were told.

They waited. They listened for a scream, but none came. Margaret spoke only of the Lord. And as the waters began to lap about her feet, she sang a verse from one of the psalms.

My sins and faults of youth
Do thou, O Lord, forget;
After thy mercy think on me,
And for thy goodness great.

Someone ran from the crowd when the girl was almost drowning. Grabbing Margaret, and holding her up above the water, he told her to say, 'God save the King.'

'God save him, if he will, for it is his salvation that I desire.'

A woman on the shore gasped out, 'There, she has said it, now let her go!'

But one man with a vicious temper snarled, 'We don't want that wench's prayers. Make her sign the Oath.'

Margaret was asked to sign the Oath and she refused.

'I will not,' she said. 'I am one of Christ's children; let me go.'

They did, and the water flowed over her head. That was when a new day began for Margaret in heaven.

Fact file:

The Killing Times: The two Margarets were killed in 1685, during a period known as the Killing Times, when there was widespread persecution of Covenanters and a great many killed, often without any trial at all. Magistrates were ordered to get everyone in their district to take the Abjuration Oath, and to kill anyone who refused. The Oath was there to get people to renounce the Covenants, which had been signed in protest at the king interfering with the church. They were forceful in their terms, however, and the government regarded them as statements of open rebellion.

Keynote: Margaret's refusal to take the Oath made her an outlaw. Normally, we think that we can always rely on the government and the law to keep us safe, but in God we have a help even more sure than that. God was with Margaret even when the forces of the law were against her, or the waves were rushing around her. God is still our refuge in time of need.

Think: The soldiers wanted Margaret to take the Abjuration Oath, but she could not do that because it meant she would be putting loyalty to the king above loyalty to God. God cannot accept anything less than being first in our hearts. Think about the things that you might be tempted to love more than God, and why he is far better than them.

Prayer: Lord Jesus, thank you for your continual protection and encouragement. Please sustain me in times of difficulty. Teach me to trust you more than anything or anyone else. Amen.

Judith Weinberg

It was the early summer of 1910, and Judith and her two younger sisters were as excited as could be.

'How many days till we go to visit Grandfather and Grandmother?' Judith asked her youngest sister, who was learning to count.

Holding up both hands the dark-haired six-year-old struggled to separate her fingers, and was eventually satisfied with the result. Judith might have laughed, but she did not. One small hand had $2\frac{1}{2}$ fingers up and the other had $3\frac{1}{2}$. Though the little girl didn't exactly mean to do that the result was the same.

'That's right' smiled Judith. 'Six days from now we'll be leaving the town and heading into the forest for the summer. Grandmother will have begun baking already. She knows how much you like her sugar ginger biscuits.'

Much though Mr Weinberg loved his three daughters, especially Judith, he was not sorry that they were going off on holiday. Summer was a busy time for his business and, in any case, Judith was going through a tiresome stage. She asked question after question after question... after question, so much so that sometimes his head was in a spin trying to keep up with her.

'How am I meant to know all the answers?' he asked his wife. 'I study the Talmud, but I'm not a Rabbi. What Judith needs is her own personal Rabbi who can take time to answer all her questions.'

'She'll have one soon,' Mrs Weinberg grinned. 'And I'm sure Grandfather Weinberg will give her the answers she's looking for.'

'I hope so,' Judith's father said, smiling, 'though he didn't always have the answers to my questions when I was growing up.'

The six days passed in a bustle of packing and repacking as the three Weinberg girls organised themselves for several weeks in the forest. Judith was more concerned about what books to take with her, and her sisters couldn't agree on which of their wooden dolls were absolutely necessary. Eventually the great day came and Judith, with her two young sisters and their mother, climbed into the horse-drawn carriage, settled themselves down, and watched as the coachman whipped the horse into action.

'We're on our way,' Judith thought silently, winging her thoughts to her grandfather. Her sisters chattered nearly every minute of the journey, and from time to time Mrs Weinberg looked at her oldest daughter and smiled.

'What a lovely girl she's growing into,' the woman thought. 'Her dark hair shines. Her brown eyes sparkle like stars. And what a nice olive complexion she has.'

Suddenly, as though Judith read her mother's thoughts, her olive skin turned pink with embarrassment. At 13 years of age, Judith was discovering what it meant to be self-conscious.

Grandfather Weinberg was all that Judith needed him to be for most of that holiday. Although he was a Rabbi, he was also a busy timber merchant. But he still made time for his grand-daughter, and he answered her questions as best he could.

'You want to know so many things!' he laughed often. 'It's as though you're training to be a woman Rabbi – and we can't have that, can we?'

Judith chose her questions carefully, and without her grandfather knowing it they were all leading to the biggest question of all. Partly out of fear of old Mr Weinberg's reaction, and partly because she was working the answer out for herself, she kept it right to the end.

'Tell me about Jesus,' the teenager asked, when she thought the right time had come. 'Who was he? And why don't we talk about him?'

There was no way that the girl could have guessed what her question would do to the grandfather she loved. The man changed colour, his face went from angry to sad to … something she could not quite work out. And it seemed a long time before he began to answer her question at all.

When she went to bed that night Judith was more confused that ever. Rather than going straight to sleep, she turned over in her mind all she knew about Jesus. He had lived about 1900 years ago. Jesus was a Jew like herself. Some people thought he was the Messiah that Jews were waiting for, but he couldn't have been because he was crucified. And Grandfather Weinberg pointed out that the Scripture said that anyone who died on a tree was cursed, and the Messiah could not be cursed. Yet, reasoned Judith, Christians believed that Jesus was the Messiah. Could Christians be right about him being the Jewish Messiah, and Jews all be wrong? It seemed very unlikely. But the thought wouldn't leave Judith alone, though she decided it was best not to broach the subject with Grandfather again.

On arriving back home after the summer, Judith used her eyes and her mind to try to answer her questions without bombarding her father with them.

'What a relief!' Mr Weinberg said, when the family had been home a week. 'Dad seems to have answered all Judith's questions after all, either that or she's run out of things to ask.'

His wife smiled. 'So it seems.'

But Judith's questions still came into her mind thick and fast. 'Why do Christians hate Jews?' she asked herself, then decided it was because Jews were involved in the trial of Jesus Christ, even though it was the Roman authorities that put him to death. But that didn't fit the facts either, because there were Christians at her school who really went out of their way to be kind to Jews. 'Why do Christians fight with each other if they all think the Messiah has come?' was another question that bothered her. Yet she could see that there were Christians in her town who really loved each other.

Four years later, in 1914, Judith and her family had to move from their home town, and they had to move quickly. Fighting had been raging in Russia for years, but now the possibility of a European war was beginning to cause a great deal of fear among those who lived, as the Weinbergs did, near the Russian-German border. Jews were especially fearful of what

111

would happen to them. Then on 1st August the worst happened. War was declared. The First World War had begun. Judith's family, like thousands of others, fled from the area near the German border. The Weinbergs, carrying all that they could of their possessions, walked for four days before boarding a crowded freight train that they hoped would take them to safety. And it seemed that was just what happened. Settling in what was thought to be a safe town, they picked up the pieces of their lives, and Mr Weinberg once again established himself in business.

Judith left many things behind in her old home, but she took her thoughts and her questions with her. It was some years before they became a real problem again.

'Solomon,' she said, to the young man she loved and to whom she was engaged to be married, 'are you very interested in religion?'

The handsome young man shrugged his shoulders. 'Not really,' he admitted, 'but I'll always be a Jew.'

'Wouldn't you like to know what Christians believe?' asked Judith.

'Not particularly,' Solomon said.

'Will you come to church with me?' she went on. 'I'd like to see what goes on there.'

That caught Solomon off guard. He thought he was very sophisticated and didn't really believe anything, but he was Jewish enough to baulk at the thought of going to a Christian meeting.... But he loved Judith and would do anything for her.

'All right, why not?' he asked. 'I'll come with you.'

Had Solomon known what would happen, he would have run a hundred miles in the opposite direction!

As a result of what she heard at the Christian meeting Judith attended with Solomon she became a Christian. Understanding her parents' reaction is difficult. When some Jewish people look back over history, they see hundreds of years when those who claimed to be Christians were their enemies. Over the centuries Jewish people have grown to fear 'Christians', though no Jew has anything to fear from someone who truly loves the Lord Jesus, who himself was Jewish.

Because the Weinbergs loved Judith deeply they tried to persuade her to change her mind. Her father talked to her, argued with her, pleaded with her. Judith's mother wept over her and tried to love her back into her Jewish faith. Even her young sisters did what they could to persuade her to give up her new beliefs. But it wasn't that easy. As a young Jewess Judith had believed in her head what she was taught, but as a Christian

113

she knew in her heart that what the Bible said was true, Jesus was her Messiah, her Saviour. And when she thought of what he had done on the cross to save her from her sin, there was no way she could give up her new-found faith just to please her family. Eventually she left home knowing that her parents would have nothing more to do with her, and that they would not allow her young sisters to keep in touch.

'Where do I go?' Judith asked, as the door of her home slammed shut behind her. And that was one question that didn't take long to answer. 'I'll go to my Christian friends.'

When she knocked on the door of her pastor's home, she was welcomed in like one of the family. And that's what she was. Before long plans were made for her to move to a different town where she could build a new life within the Christian community.

'Are you going to the meeting tonight?' a friend asked, not long after she had settled in her new home.

'Yes, I am,' Judith replied. 'I've heard about the speaker and I'm really looking forward to hearing more about the work he's doing.'

That night Judith listened with her heart as well as her mind as the speaker described the work he did.

'We travel from town to town, from village to village, telling people about Jesus.'

Judith could picture herself doing just that, after all she already visited people in her spare time to talk about her faith.

'The work isn't easy,' the man continued. 'Sometimes we have to walk miles in the cold Russian weather. And I remember times when I've not been in dry clothes for days at a time.'

Looking at her warm dry clothes, Judith knew that she wouldn't even mind being cold and wet if the people she spoke to trusted the Lord.

'There are days when we eat very little, and occasionally nothing at all,' said the man. 'But for all the hardships, I wonder if there is anyone here who will join us in the work.'

Silence filled the church for an uncomfortably long time, before a quiet and steady voice said, 'I am willing to answer the call of the Lord.'

It was Judith.

The work she began soon afterwards was just as it had been described. With the little groups of missionaries she travelled in all kinds of weather. The speaker had told the truth. Her clothes often didn't dry out by morning, and there were times when her empty rumbling tummy tried to keep her awake at night. But Judith loved it! The rain didn't matter and the mud didn't bother her. She even thought it was a privilege to be hungry in order to serve Jesus.

One day Judith knocked at the door of the last house in a poor little village. When there was no reply, she pushed the door open and could hardly take in what she saw. Several orphaned children were lying unconscious from typhus fever. Rolling up her sleeves, she nursed the children, cleaned their filthy home, and did all she could. So it was no surprise when she caught typhus herself. The only surprise was that she recovered from it after being very near to death. Just as soon as she was well enough, Judith was back at work once again. She never tired of talking of Jesus.

'Why does the name Jesus make the soldiers so full of rage?' she asked the mission leader, when she was spat on.

'They hate the name of Jesus,' the old man explained. 'They think that religion is just a way of deceiving people.'

'Don't they know that Jesus is the Truth, that he won't deceive anyone?'

'No, my child,' was the reply. 'That's what we're here to tell them.'

It was autumn and the evenings were short. On her way home from visiting, Judith just loved kicking the dry autumn leaves, and feeling them crunch under her feet. It reminded her of times in the forest with Grandfather. As she walked, she prayed for her family whom she still loved though they would have nothing to do with her.

The mood of a group of soldiers in the village grew uglier and uglier every time they heard the missionaries telling people about Jesus. And for some reason their rage overflowed when they thought of Judith. One day she was arranging a meeting in another village nearby when the soldiers lost control of themselves. Barging into the meeting she was leading, they grabbed the young woman, accusing her of terrible things. Having seen murders before, the villagers left the meeting and slid into the relative safety of their own homes. The last they saw of Judith was when she was marched – surrounded by soldiers with their swords held high – to a barn near the end of the village. Her body was found the next day with her Bible right beside her. News of Judith's murder spread through the village like wildfire.

'She loved us with Jesus' love,' an old woman told her husband.

Tears prevented an answer. The man just nodded his head in agreement.

And as they grieved together, Judith enjoyed to the full the wonderful love of Jesus.

Fact file:

 Jewish Diaspora: In Jesus' day, most Jews lived in Israel, although some had moved away (like the Apostle Paul's family). By Judith's time, however, very few of the people living in Israel were Jewish. Around 70 AD, the Jewish people tried to overthrow their Roman rulers, but they were unsuccessful. The Romans were not pleased about this and their army destroyed the Temple and scattered a great many Jews throughout the known world. Many of them suffered a lot of prejudice and persecution for years. They were sometimes forced to wear special badges, marking them as Jews, and to live in areas called ghettos. This scattering of Jews is sometimes called the 'Jewish Diaspora'.

 Keynote: When Judith decided to become a Christian, her family expelled her. Things like this can be very difficult and painful, but Jesus warned us that such things would happen (Matthew 10:34-39). Jesus understands what it feels like because his own family thought he was mad (Mark 3:21). He also promises to look after us. We find a new family amongst his people because we become part of God's family.

Think: Judith was keen to tell other people about Jesus, but that did not stop her from giving practical help when that was what was needed. Judith knew that people had a body as well as a soul. In fact, her practical help probably made people more willing to listen to what she had to say. Can you think of any ways in which you could help people practically?

Prayer: Lord Jesus, thank you for the good news that is available for everyone, whatever their background. Help me to love and help people because they need it, rather than because of any benefit I hope to get myself. Amen.

Betty Stam

It was winter and very, very cold. In fact, it was as cold as it could be at the beginning of winter in China. Betty Scott could hardly move. She was dressed in full Chinese winter clothes. All you could see was padded, and what you couldn't see was padded too.

'I can hardly bend at the knees,' she laughed. 'And my elbows won't bend either.'

Her mother smiled.

'I'm sure if I gave you some nuts you'd manage to get them into your mouth!'

Betty grinned. 'I guess I would.'

'Chinese winter clothes always feel so bulky when you first put them on, but you'll soon get used to them.'

'I remember that from last year,' eight-year-old Betty said. 'Then in the spring, when I went back to ordinary clothes, I felt like a butterfly coming out of a chrysalis!'

Dr Charles Scott, Betty's father, smiled at the thought of his heavily-padded eldest child becoming a butterfly.

'You say the most extraordinary things,' he commented. 'In fact, you're really quite a poet.'

Betty grinned. She loved writing poems, and she knew her parents liked the ones she showed them.

Looking at her well-padded sisters and little brother, Betty wondered what life was like for her cousins far away in America. Were they waddling around in padded clothes?

Dr Scott smiled at the thought.

'I guess it's very different for them,' he said. 'And you'll discover that for yourself when you go back to America for college.'

Betty shook her head. 'I left America when I was six months old,' she laughed. 'China's my home, and I'll go to college here then marry and have my own children right here.'

Then she laughed. 'And I'll pad them all up each winter and pack them in a drawer until the summer comes again! They'll not feel the cold that way.'

'I think it's time we were leaving for church,' Dr Scott said. 'And we'll delay discussion on your adult life until you're at least ten years old!'

That seemed a good idea to Betty, who waddled down the street towards the church where she knew her Chinese friends would be waiting for her. A girl and boy came along the road to meet her, and she immediately changed from speaking English to her dad to speaking in a Chinese dialect to her friends. It happened without Betty realizing what she was doing as she was perfectly at home using both languages.

Although Betty wanted to stay in China all her life she didn't quite know where. Her earliest memories were of Tsingtao in the province of Shantung. But when she finished primary school in Tsingtao, and went to boarding school in Tungchow, her family moved to Tsinan. The first time she went home on holiday to Tsinan was very strange.

'I know it's home,' she told her family, 'because you are all here. But it's very odd going into the street and not seeing any faces I recognise. I really miss seeing my old friends.'

Mrs Scott understood Betty's sadness and made a point of introducing her to some girls her age that attended church. Because Betty found it easy to write down her feelings, several times that holiday her parents discovered her curled up in a sunny corner with her notebook of poems. Before her first holiday in Tsinan was over, Betty was beginning to feel that it was really becoming home.

'Would you like to read us some of your poems?' Dr Scott asked one evening, after they had eaten and before the last of the sunlight faded.

Betty flicked back through the pages.

'Here's one I wrote when I was ten,' she said, and then settled down to read it.

> *I cannot live like Jesus*
> *Example though he be*
> *For he was strong and selfless*
> *And I am tied to me.*
>
> *I cannot live like Jesus*
> *My soul is never free*
> *My will is strong and stubborn*
> *My love is weak and wee.*
> *But I have asked my Jesus*
> *To live his life in me.*
>
> *I cannot look like Jesus*
> *More beautiful is he*
> *In soul and eye and stature*
> *Than sunrise on the sea.*

And before she was able to read the last few lines a cloud went over the setting sun and it was too dark to continue reading her tiny handwriting.

An hour later it was completely dark. Betty's two little sisters and two little brothers were sound asleep in bed and she was still wide awake. Instead of tossing and turning she rose and felt her way through to the living-room where her parents were reading by the light of a Chinese lantern.

'In you come and join us,' Dr Scott said. 'We don't often have you all to ourselves.'

Betty curled up beside her mother and felt loved.

'That was a beautiful poem you read us,' Dr Scott said softly. 'Can you remember how it finishes?'

Screwing up her eyes, Betty tried to remember but couldn't.

'No,' she said. 'It's ages since I've read that one. But it ends with a couple of lines about how those who believe in Jesus will be just like him when they go home to heaven.'

'That will be a wonderful day,' said Mrs Scott.

The three of them talked for a long time that night. But when Betty went back to bed it was that great day when she would go to heaven and be like Jesus that came into her mind. Although she didn't sleep for quite a while, her thoughts were so full of the wonder of being like the Lord that being awake in the middle of the night didn't seem to matter at all.

When Betty was 17 years old, in 1923, her parents were due to go back to America on home leave. Betty had been back before, but this time was different for she was going to remain in America to attend Wilson College in Pennsylvania. Although she'd been away in boarding school for several years, the thought of being on the opposite side of the world from her parents was a very odd one. Sometimes the thought of it ate at her heart.

'We've decided to travel home to America by the scenic route,' Dr Scott told Betty, as they planned to leave China for their time of home leave. 'In fact, we're going to have really quite an exciting journey!'

Betty thought that the route of one long sea voyage would be much the same as the route of another. After all, what difference would it make which sea they passed through, they were all wet, wavy and some shade of blue.

Dr Scott continued what he was saying. 'We're going to America by way of Palestine, Egypt, Greece, Italy, France and England.'

Now, Betty was a very lady-like seventeen-year-old, so it was more than a little unusual to see her with her mouth wide open as through she were catching flies!

'Is that a surprise?' her father asked.

Realising that her mouth was open, Betty closed it ... then opened it again to say just one word. 'Wow!'

The journey back home to America was all Betty imagined it would be. When she wasn't answering the younger children's questions about the places they travelled through, she was asking her parents questions or looking up things in the guidebooks they carried with them. By the time they arrived in America Betty felt more able to cope with being left there. After all, she had travelled the world... or a very large part of it!

China was never far from Betty Scott's mind. Every single day she pictured what her parents would be doing, imagining her sisters at boarding school and her two young brothers still at home. Before falling asleep she often imagined herself back in China, and sometimes if she woke in the night she was almost surprised to find herself in her room at Wilson College.

Having become a Christian as a child, Betty was very involved in Christian activities at college right from the start. Her letters home encouraged her parents because she wrote of the Christian friends she made and the meetings she attended. One letter in particular, written in 1925, gave them special joy.

'I've just returned from a conference in New Jersey,' she wrote. 'I've had such a wonderful time, and I've rededicated my life to the Lord. He seemed to speak to me really directly, telling me that after college I should prepare to be a missionary — that he wants me back home in China!'

Betty knew what she should do with her life, but how was she to do it? First, she knew she had to work hard at college and get a good degree. And while she was doing that she found out about missionary training colleges and decided that the right place for her to go was the famous Moody Bible Institute in Chicago. Thousands of missionaries had done their training there, and the thought of joining them was very exciting. She might have been even more excited had she known that God was sending a young man to Moody who would become very special to her. John Stam had intended to go into business, but God had another plan for his life. He found himself, just seven years after he was converted, heading for Moody Bible Institute. Betty and John met and became fond of each other. It's hard to imagine how they felt in the summer of 1931 when Betty graduated and prepared to sail for China to serve the Lord with China Inland Mission.

'I'll follow you next summer,' John promised, thinking how long his last year at Moody would seem without the girl he loved.

'And if we still feel the same about each other after we've worked in China for a while we'll get married,' Betty reminded him.

As her ship nudged away from the docks, John's mind was in a spin. China seemed so far away. When would they meet again? After all,

China was a big place, and they could be at opposite sides of the country. Would Betty still love him in a few years' time?

Having watched her ship until it was just a blur on the ocean, John spun round and walked away. He didn't know the answers to his questions, but he knew someone who did. As he walked he talked to God, and Betty was talking to him too. The one thing they were both sure of was that the Lord understood what they were feeling.

In October 1932, Betty had to go to Shanghai for medical treatment and to visit her parents. She was still there on the day that John's ship arrived. Scanning the crowds for a face that might belong to a fellow-missionary, he had the nicest surprise of his life when the one missionary he knew in China grinned back at him. It was Betty!

And did they still feel the same way about each other? Nobody who saw them meeting that day would have needed to ask that question! Very soon they became engaged, then after a year of language study and working in different places, John and Betty were married.

Were they the happiest people in the whole wide world? They certainly felt it. And their happiness was complete the following autumn when their little daughter was born. They called her Helen Priscilla.

'My sister Helen will like that,' Betty said, stroking her baby's soft cheek and looking deep into her baby-blue eyes.

Just a few weeks after Helen's birth, her parents took her to Tsingteh.

'Haven't missionaries been evacuated from there in the past?' a friend asked, when she heard where they were going.

'Yes,' Betty admitted. 'But it seems to be safe from the Communists just now. In any case, the local magistrate has guaranteed our safety from Communist attack.'

Her friend still looked worried. 'Look,' Betty said, 'Communists are everywhere, and if we think about them we'll be frightened out of our wits. But if we remember that we are safe in the hands of Almighty God, we'll cope whatever happens.' She believed with all her heart that was true.

On 6th December 1934, Tsingteh suffered a sudden and totally unexpected attack from Communist forces, and the city fell. It was early morning when Betty heard what all the noise was about, while she was in the middle of bathing little Helen. John and Betty knelt with their Chinese friends and prayed for God's will to be done.

'Would you like tea?' Betty asked the Communists, much to their surprise, when they arrived to interrogate John.

But the tea and the kindness did nothing to soften their hard hearts. John was tied to a chair and taken away. Before Betty had time to think what was happening to her husband, his captors came back and took her and Helen too.

'Don't follow us,' Betty urged the servants. 'They'll shoot you if you do.' Then in a whisper, she added, 'If they kill us please look out for Helen.'

Later that day John was allowed back to collect some things, and he too comforted their broken-hearted friends.

The following day John, Betty and Helen were taken twelve miles over the mountains to Miaosheo. It is hard to write about what happened next, but only a few words will tell the story. On 8th December, Betty and John were beheaded, and the instant that happened they met Jesus face to face in heaven. Three-month-old Helen was left alone in a house to die. And it was there that she was found, thirty hours later, by a Christian friend. Snug in her Chinese padded sleeping-bag, and none the worse of her lack of food, little Helen Stam was unharmed. The Lord, who had taken her parents home to heaven, took care of the little girl he left behind. As a child Betty thought it would be a long time till she saw Jesus. But it wasn't very long after all.

Fact file:

 China: By the time that Betty was born, China had been a country for longer than any other state that was still in existence. Recorded history in China reaches back to around 1736 BC. When European travellers first went there, they were astonished to discover paper money, which was not known in Europe at the time. The Chinese are also credited with inventing gunpowder and building the only man-made structure visible from the moon – the Great Wall of China.

 Keynote: Even when Betty realised that she would not be able to look after her baby, she knew that God would. And God did. It is amazing to think that such a young baby could survive without any care or food for so long. God is able to care for all of his children, even when they cannot care for themselves.

Think: John must have been worried when he arrived in Shanghai for the first time. It was a huge country, and he had never been there before in his life. God sent the one person he most wanted to see to meet him. God is very kind to us in his providence, running the whole universe very smoothly and sometimes giving us happy surprises that we don't expect. Can you think of some of the ways in which God has been kind to you?

 Prayer: Lord Jesus, you are a great God who is in charge of the whole world. Thank you for caring for people like me. Please help me to care for those around me every day. Amen.

Esther John

Qamar Zea was eight years old and busy at work. Crouched on the ground outside her home in South India, she was picking her way through the fruit that had been gathered the previous day.

'Take out the bruised fruits and we'll use them right away,' her mother said. 'And don't leave any bruised ones in the basket or all of them will rot.'

The child did as she was told, but she cast longing eyes at her brothers who were heading off to play.

Noticing where her daughter was looking, Qamar Zea's mother shook her head.

'Girls are never children,' she thought. 'Indian boys have a childhood when they can run and play with their friends, but the girls work from as soon as they're able.'

'There is so much fruit to go through,' the child moaned, looking at the flat basket piled high.

'Just you be grateful that we live in a part of India where there is enough rain to make the fruit grow,' the woman said, impatient to get back to her cooking. 'Further north there's nothing but dryness and dust.'

Looking at the greenness of the area in which she lived, Qamar Zea sighed then set about the job she had to do, knowing that when she was finished another one would be waiting for her.

Before many more years had passed the girl often helped her mother with the cooking. She enjoyed that as it gave them time to talk together.

'I don't understand,' Qamar Zea said one day. It was a Friday. 'Why is it that on Fridays when the men in our family go to the mosque to worship Allah, most of the other men in the village spend the day working?'

'That's life in India,' said her mother. 'It is a land of three peoples. Most are Hindu. They worship many gods, so many gods I don't know how they know who to worship in what day of the week.'

The girl looked shocked. 'But God the Lord is one God,' she said, having been taught the Koran, even though as a Muslim girl she was rarely inside a mosque. 'And who are the other two peoples?' she asked, fascinated.

'There are Christians in South India,' her mother explained. 'And there have been for
136

hundreds of years. It's said that one of the Prophet Jesus' disciples came to Kerela and told the people about his Master.'

'And there are Muslims like us,' said Qamar Zea, 'who know that God the Lord is one God and that he is Allah, and that Jesus is one of his prophets.'

The woman smiled.

'Shh, girl, and stir the stew. You're training to be a cook not a Muslim teacher.'

Qamar Zea was privileged because she attended school. Not all girls in her village went, although most boys did. During her eighth class in the government school her father became seriously ill and she had to stop school for a time. When he recovered she went to a Christian school, which was more convenient for her home.

'I've never known anyone like our teacher before,' she told one of her new friends. 'She speaks to us in such a gentle way and she's so kind to all her pupils.'

Watching this woman carefully made a great impression on Qamar Zea.

'How can a person be like her?' she asked herself. 'She does her work so well and lives a better life than anyone else I know. I wonder what makes her so different.'

This was particularly surprising to the Muslim teenager as she had been brought up to believe that Christians were blasphemers who spoke against Allah, and not good people at all.

'Don't let your teachers tell you lies about Allah,' the girl was warned, by the men in her family.

Qamar Zea held her peace. None of her family knew that two days each week she studied Old Testament in school, two days she studied New Testament, and on the fifth day she learned Bible verses by memory.

'Christians believe that there is only one God,' she thought, as she studied. 'But they believe that Jesus is God rather than just one of the prophets. I'm confused.'

Not long afterwards, on one of the days for memorising Bible verses, the girls in her class were given part of Isaiah 53 to learn. Qamar Zea read the verses over and over again as she tried to remember them. 'We all, like sheep, have gone astray, each one of us has turned to his own way; and the Lord has laid on him the iniquity of us all.'

Later she explained what happened that day.

'We were memorising some parts of Isaiah 53, which was very hard for me. Then I began to realise that Jesus is alive for ever. Thus God put faith in my heart and I believed in Jesus as my Saviour and the forgiver of my sins. Only he could save me from everlasting death. That was when I began to realise
138

how great a sinner I was, whereas before I thought my good life could save me.'

Now for a 60 word history lesson. The landmass that is now India, Bangladesh and Pakistan used to be all part of India. In 1947 it split into three parts: India, East Pakistan and West Pakistan. East Pakistan eventually changed its name to Bangladesh. The main reason for this split was religious. The new India was mainly Hindu, and Pakistan was set up as a Muslim state. That was exactly 60 words; check it if you like!

When the Muslim state of Pakistan was founded, Qamar Zea's family moved northwest to live there. They settled in the city of Karachi. She was 18 years old.

'Are you Qamar Zea?' a stranger asked the young woman one day.

'Yes,' she answered. 'But who are you?'

'I'm a Christian friend,' the woman explained. 'My name is Miss Laugesen, and some Christians in India have asked me to do anything I can to help you.'

Qamar Zea smiled.

'Is there anything you need?' the woman asked.

'Just one thing,' said Qamar Zea. 'Would it be possible for you to get me a New Testament?'

The Christian worker brought her a New Testament under cover of darkness, because it would have caused terrible trouble in Qamar Zea's family if she had been found out.

It was seven years before she would meet Miss Laugesen again, and it was at a time of deep trouble for Qamar Zea.

'My family have planned a Muslim marriage for me,' the young Christian explained, when she arrived at Miss Laugesen's home. 'That's why I've come to you.'

The Christian worker welcomed the girl and they set up home together.

It wasn't long before Qamar Zea's brothers found out where she was, and followed her.

'Come home with us,' they demanded. 'Your father has a good marriage partner for you.'

'No,' their sister said quietly. 'I cannot come.'

But her brothers persuaded her to return to see her mother. She did, but was soon back in the safety of Miss Laugesen's home. From there she went north to Sahiwal in the Punjab where she worked in a Christian hospital. During her time in Sahiwal she was baptised as a Christian believer and took a new name, Esther John.

'I feel God wants me to be a teacher of the Bible,' she explained at her baptism. 'This book has great power. I want to see it do for others what it has done for me.'

In 1956, the brave young woman began a completely new stage of her life. She left Sahiwal and went to the city of Gujranwala, to attend the United Bible Training Centre in order to train as a Bible teacher. For a Muslim family like hers it was a disgrace that she had become a Christian, but even more so when she went to train as a Bible teacher. Esther John's brothers were enraged at what she had done, and no doubt her mother wept many tears.

The United Bible Training Centre is a residential centre then run by missionaries from America and Britain. Within the compound there was a building with a central courtyard where Esther John lived with other women who were training to be Bible teachers. Each day began with worship in the small chapel. Then they had classes in which they studied the Bible, but they also learned practical things like cooking and ordering food. For recreation they went out on the lawn where they played games, skipped and did things Esther John and the other students hadn't had the opportunity to do as children at home. One of the fun activities was done for a serious reason, and that was learning to ride a bicycle. This was very unusual for Pakistani girls. As part of her training, each girl cycled to local villages with a missionary. There they gathered the women for Bible reading, prayer and singing, and on

141

other occasions they taught Bible stories to the children. Saturdays and Sundays were different. Saturdays were busy with cleaning, laundry, hair-washing and preparation for the next day. Then on Sundays they went to the local church and often returned home to the United Bible Training Centre for some hymn singing and reading. After her busy week, Esther John enjoyed her quiet Sundays.

Following three years of training, Esther John left Gujranwala and moved to the little town of Chichawatni.

'I would like you to live in our home with us,' a Christian worker called Mrs Dale White told her.

And that's what Esther John did.

'Chichawatni is my lovely home,' she said, smiling, as she looked around the shady well-watered compound with its brightly coloured flowering trees. Then she laughed, 'And as Chichawatni is now my home, I'm going to dress as the women here do.'

Until then Esther John had continued wearing her Indian sari. Getting dressed each day was very different from then on as she put on her baggy trousers and shalwar chemise (long tunic top). Finally she had always to wear the daputta that covered her head and shoulders. The outfit was not complete without the daputta, as in a Muslim country it was not proper for a woman to show bare skin.

142

Not only did the new Bible teacher surprise her friends by wearing Pakistani clothes, she amazed the people of Chichawatni by riding her bicycle!

'Look at her!' people said, pointing in Esther John's direction. 'What next?'

And there was a next.... that was the Punjabi language. If ever a young woman was determined to do all she could to spread the good news that Jesus Christ is the one and only Saviour, Esther John was that young woman. With Mrs White she travelled from village to village and town to town to speak to any women who would listen. And many did. Muslim women were often restricted to their own homes or compounds, but somehow God opened the way for these two intrepid missionaries to meet them there.

'You still have the light of the holy Prophet Muhammad in your face!' one Muslim woman told Esther John.

'It's the light of Jesus,' the Bible woman explained. 'It is he who is my Saviour, and it is he who makes my face shine.'

'But how could you leave your Muslim background?' she was asked, over and over again.

'God's grace was upon me,' was her often repeated reply.

Then with a smiling face, and a great deal of enthusiasm, she shared the story of Jesus in word, picture and song.

143

'Let's prepare a special play for Christmas,' she said to the children in Chichawatni.

From then on every spare minute was spent doing just that, amid much fun and laughter.

But there was a shadow over Esther John's life, as her family had begun sending her frequent letters asking her to return home. The thought disturbed her, but eventually she agreed to go at the end of the year on two conditions.

'I must be allowed to live as a Christian,' she wrote home, 'and I must not be forced into a Muslim marriage.'

'I sent that letter by registered mail,' she told Mrs White, some time later, 'but I've had no reply.'

Because of that Esther John was unwilling to go home to her family, so she arranged to go off on mission with the Whites for a month before returning to her much-loved Chichawatni.

On the evening of her return, Esther John sang happily as she polished her pots and pans. Having a slight cold she went off to bed early. The house was full of guests, which is perhaps why the intruder was not heard. But there was an intruder, and he only did one thing. Nothing was stolen, nothing was disturbed, but Esther John was attacked and murdered. She was not the first Muslim convert to die because she had dared to become a Christian, and she will not be the last. Muslims in Chichawatni joined Christians at Esther John's funeral. Of course the police were called in and they investigated the murder. The result of their investigations was a wonderful tribute to a lovely lady. 'Sir,' they told Mr White, 'we have found no clue. This girl was in love only with your Christ.'

Although the Whites grieved for their friend, they knew she was in heaven with Jesus whom she loved best of all.

Fact file:

 Names: We don't normally think about names very much, but in the past they were seen as very important. In the Bible we are often given the reason for someone's name when they are born. Many people changed their names when they became Christians because their old names sometimes referred to heathen gods. This practice was so common in Britain in the past that we often call a person's first name their Christian name.

 Keynote: Qamar Zea had been brought up to think that she could please God by being good, but as she learned the verses from Isaiah, she learned she was a great sinner in God's eyes and only Jesus could save her from her sins. When we look around us, we might think that we are doing not too badly, but we have to look to the Bible to find God's standard and God's solution.

Think: Qamar Zea was very impressed by the gentleness of her teacher in the Christian school. She was so impressed that she wanted to know how she could live like her teacher. Her teacher was following Jesus' command to be a light in the world and to love her neighbour. It had a great effect! How do you think you could show the same gentleness and kindness?

Prayer: Lord Jesus, I know that I am a sinner, and that I can't save myself with lots of good deeds. Thank you for offering salvation through your free grace and forgiveness. Please help me to show something of the gentleness and kindness that you command us to show. Amen.

Quiz

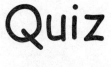

How much can you remember about the ten girls who didn't give in? Try answering these questions to find out.

Blandina

1. What was Blandina's mum doing when she was playing tig with her friend?

2. Which city in Gaul did Blandina live in?

3. Which words from the preacher always gave Blandina a warm feeling?

Perpetua

4. Where is Carthage?

5. Which book of the Bible did Felicitas refer to when she was waiting to go into the arena?

6. What do the names Perpetua and Felicitas mean when you put them together?

Lady Jane Grey

7. Which king of England had the Dowager Queen been married to?

8. What relation was Jane to Queen Mary?

9. Who tried to make Jane queen and his son king?

Anne Askew

10. How did Anne's tutor describe the sea?

11. Why did she have to marry Thomas Kyme instead of her sister?

12. How was Anne tortured to try and make her change her mind?

Lysken Dirks

13. Which town did Lysken live in when she married?

14. What did the guards find that Jeronius had written?

15. Why did the authorities kill Lysken early?

Marion Harvey

16. Which Firth is Bo-ness on?

17. Which preacher was Marion arrested for going to hear?

18. What did her friend think that he preached about and what did he really preach about?

Margaret Wilson

19. What was Margaret's father's job?

20. How did the people at the meal notice Margaret and her sister?

21. Which town is near the place where they drowned?

Judith Weinberg

22. What position did Judith's grandfather hold, apart from being a timber merchant?

23. Which war began in 1914?

24. What was wrong with the children that Judith nursed?

Betty Stam

25. What did Betty say she felt like when she got into her summer clothes?

26. Where did Betty go to train to be a missionary?

27. What did Betty offer the Communists when they arrived?

Esther John

28. Which part of India did Qamar Zea's mother tell her that the Christians lived in?

29. What did the name of East Pakistan eventually change to?

30. What did Esther give up wearing when she moved to Chicawatni?

How well did you do?

Turn over to find out...

Answers

1. Drawing water from a well

2. Lyon

3. 'Brothers and sisters'

4. North Africa

5. Revelation

6. Everlasting Happiness

7. Henry VIII

8. Her cousin

9. Dudley

10. Like the River Witham over and over again

11. Her sister died before the wedding

12. She was stretched on the rack

13. Antwerp

14. A poem

15. To prevent a scene

16. The Firth of Forth

17. Donald Cargill

18. She thought that he preached about fire and brimstone but he really preached about the love of God.

19. He was a farmer

20. They didn't drink to the King's health

21. Wigton

22. He was a Rabbi

23. The First World War

24. They had typhus fever

25. A butterfly

26. Moody Bible Institute

27. Tea

28. The South

29. Bangladesh

30. The Indian Sari

Start collecting this series now!

Ten Boys who Didn't Give In

Polycarp

Alban

Sir John Oldcastle

Thomas Cramer

George Wishart

James Chalmers

Dietrich Bonhoeffer

Nate Saint

Ivan Moiseyev

Graham Staines

ISBN 1-84550-0350

Ten Boys who Changed the World
David Livingstone, Billy Graham, Brother Andrew, John Newton, William Carey, George Müller, Nicky Cruz, Eric Liddell, Luis Palau, Adoniram Judson.
ISBN 1-85792-5793

Ten Girls who Changed the World
Corrie Ten Boom, Mary Slessor, Joni Eareckson Tada, Isobel Kuhn, Amy Carmichael, Elizabeth Fry, Evelyn Brand, Gladys Aylward, Catherine Booth, Jackie Pullinger
ISBN 1-85792-6498

Ten Boys who Made a Difference
Augustine of Hippo, Jan Hus, Martin Luther, Ulrich Zwingli, William Tyndale, Hugh Latimer, John Calvin, John Knox, Lord Shaftesbury, Thomas Chalmers.
ISBN 1-85792-7753

Ten Girls who Made a Difference
Monica of Thagaste, Catherine Luther, Susanna Wesley, Ann Judson, Maria Taylor, Susannah Spurgeon, Bethan Lloyd-Jones, Edith Schaeffer, Sabina Wurmbrand, Ruth Bell Graham.
ISBN 1-85792-7761

Ten Boys who Made History
Charles Spurgeon, Jonathan Edwards, Samuel Rutherford, D L Moody, Martin Lloyd Jones, A W Tozer, John Owen, Robert Murray McCheyne, Billy Sunday, George Whitfield.
ISBN 1-85792-8369

Ten Girls who Made History
Ida Scudder, Betty Green, Jeanette Li, Mary Jane Kinnaird, Bessie Adams, Emma Dryer, Lottie Moon, Florence Nightingale, Henrietta Mears, Elisabeth Elliot.
ISBN 1-85792-8377

CHRISTIAN FOCUS

Staying Faithful - Reaching Out!

Christian Focus Publications publishes books for adults and children under its three main imprints: Christian Focus, Mentor and Christian Heritage. Our books reflect that God's word is reliable and Jesus is the way to know him, and live for ever with him.

Our children's publication list includes a Sunday school curriculum that covers pre-school to early teens; puzzle and activity books. We also publish personal and family devotional titles, biographies and inspirational stories that children will love.

If you are looking for quality Bible teaching for children then we have an excellent range of Bible story and age specific theological books.

From pre-school to teenage fiction, we have it covered!

Find us at our web page:
www.christianfocus.com